Praise for *Wild Mercy*

"*Wild Mercy* is a visitation, a chance to bask in the presence of feminine mystics, saints, and the spiritual powers from across time and space. And one can't shake the feeling that they too peer back at us through the pages of this prophetic treatise, steeping us in their friendship and blessing and tilting our hearts entirely towards the Holy One within. On every page Mirabai reminds us that women need no spiritual authority to connect us to our natural wisdom stream, no special permission to embrace the fullness of our humanity with the fullness of our divinity. And she reorients the soul completely towards this birthright."

VERA DE CHALAMBERT
author of "Kali Takes America: I'm With Her"

"An exquisite and inspiring book that reveals the great heart and wisdom of the feminine."

ROSHI JOAN JIKO HALIFAX
abbot of Upaya Zen Center and author of *Standing at the Edge*

"*Wild Mercy* is more than just a great read. It's also a magic potion, a seduction, and a bridge to a land you may not even know exists, but I am telling you, it's a very healing and inspiring place indeed. And for a book about mysticism, it's also down-to-earth and funny—such a winning combination."

ELIZABETH LESSER
cofounder of the Omega Institute and author of *The Seeker's Guide*, *Broken Open*, and *Marrow*

"Ours is a time of spiritual reclamation: reclaiming the body as holy, reclaiming the Mother as God, reclaiming the fluidity of spirit so long dammed up by the rigidity of denominated souls. Spiritual reclamation is great and good work, and as with all such work, we need a guide to point the way. Mirabai Starr is our guide, and *Wild Mercy* is our roadmap. Each chapter is an invitation to fall into the arms of the Beloved and find yourself embracing and embraced. Savor this book. Live this book."

RABBI RAMI SHAPIRO
author of *Holy Rascals: Advice for Spiritual Revolutionaries*

"What I love most about all of Mirabai Starr's work, including the magical new *Wild Mercy*, is that she writes with such joyful energy about all facets of spirituality, through a passionately feminine lens. She writes about truth, her gravest loss and most profound resurrections, infinite joy, and the stillness at the center of all things. In *Wild Mercy*, she turns her encyclopedic knowledge of all wisdom traditions and rituals to the women mystics and saints she so loves and lives by, to Mother Earth, to the mothers of all ages and genders who have nourished and guided and comforted us, and given us life, joy, the deepest healing, and a lot of light to see by."

ANNE LAMOTT
author of *Hallelujah Anyway* and *Help, Thanks, Wow*

"No one can take us into the fiery and tender depths of the sacred feminine with more skill, humor, clarity, and vibrant naked honesty than Mirabai Starr. Mirabai is herself a woman mystic grounded in the universal mysticism. The Mother is birthing in our world and her witness to what is needed in our time is essential for both men and women. I love this book, and anyone who comes to it with an open heart will find its gorgeous writing. A depth of mystical insight and wonderful practical ways to help us all live a more embodied and passionately compassionate life."

ANDREW HARVEY
author of *The Hope: A Guide to Sacred Activism*
and *The Return of the Mother*

"If you think *Wild Mercy* is just another book on feminine wisdom, Kali or Rabia or Teresa of Ávila will shake you awake ferociously and facetiously as you dance, weep, and reverently ponder the profundity in its pages. A book of poetry, of prose, of practices, of prayer, *Wild Mercy* is a sumptuous feast of Inter-Spiritual/Inter-Being that guides the reader through irreverent reverence, heartbreak, sensuality, joy, and ecstasy. The mystic in every woman craves the holy juiciness with which Mirabai tantalizes and teaches us in this extraordinary book."

CAROLYN BAKER
author of *Collapsing Consciously: Transformative Truths for Turbulent Times* and coauthor with Andrew Harvey of *Savage Grace: Living Resiliently In The Dark Night of The Globe*

"Mirabai has combined her extraordinary life experiences with her sharp intellect and her ecstatic heart to produce a book that is electrifying. She uses interviews, history, and her uniquely clear writing skills to reveal seemingly disparate world spiritual views as emanations of the wondrous and mysterious wholeness. Highly recommended!"

GANGAJI
author of *Hidden Treasure, The Diamond in Your Pocket,* and *Freedom and Resolve*

"*Wild Mercy* is a gentle and intimate portrait of the feminine mystic. In lyrical language, Mirabai Starr draws the reader into the depth of her heart as she explores the ways in which the feminine divine lives in her and with us. Sensitive to the sanctity of life, she opens herself to the wisdom of embodiment, the holiness of the everyday, and our capacity to dismantle painful structures in order to embrace suffering and to welcome the Divine Feminine Presence in our midst. It is like walking beside a close friend to feel the beating wings of mercy and the flowering heart of forgiveness. A beautiful meditation!"

BEVERLY LANZETTA
author of *The Monk Within: Embracing a Sacred Way of Life* and *Radical Wisdom: A Feminist Mystical Theology*

"In a time when we sorely need the depth and sensitivity of the feminine, Mirabai Starr guides us through the lineage of female mystics in a way that is personal, universal, and useful. I urge men to read this book as well as women, for *Wild Mercy* will open the more enduring qualities we need to begin to repair the world."

MARK NEPO
author of *More Together Than Alone* and *The Book of Awakening*

"*Wild Mercy* is the cry of so many women today as we reclaim the sacredness of form and physicality, freeing our world from the error of denigrating this holy realm of Earth. Mirabai Starr deftly shows how the natural community gathering and the wisdom of women is the way forward for our world, as the feminine voice speaks out the hidden truths and the injustices of old that are ever so reluctant to die. This book is a call for each person to take up their spiritual, creative, and activist role, as they are soulfully inspired. Thank you, Mirabai, for writing what we know to be true. May the cry of the feminine finally be heard and the doorway of the future be flung open wide!"

MEGHAN DON
author of *The New Divine Feminine: Spiritual Evolution for a Woman's Soul*

"Here is the heart's story of divine love, told in the language, the poetry, the images of the great mystics, and yet also recounted by a woman of today, someone who has lived this passion, beauty and grief in the world around us. We learn of bliss and abandonment; of being broken open by desire, sadness, and longing; of the journey back to our soul's Beloved. Embracing the wisdom of the feminine, Mirabai Starr allows us to recognize it in our body—felt in a lover's touch. And how this love reaches out, to include all of life, especially our suffering Earth. Let this book open you to the mystery of what it means to be fully alive and know love."

LLEWELLYN VAUGHAN-LEE, PHD
Sufi teacher and author of *Love is a Fire: The Sufi's Mystical Journey Home*

"More than a book, wise woman Mirabai Starr has given us the gifts of Sangha and answered prayers. Guiding us across spiritual traditions into the inspiring and sacred companionship of women teachers, pilgrims and prophets, the author reveals her own infinitely full and discerning heart with poetry, humor, and visionary wisdom. Between these pages awaits a gorgeous journey to the missing half of everything, the feminine expression of Ultimate Reality, awakening within you and in the world."

PHYLLIS CUROTT
one of America's first public Wiccan priestesses and
bestselling author of *Book of Shadows* and *Wicca Made
Easy: Awaken the Divine Magic Within You*

"*Wild Mercy* is a celebration of wisdom wherever it is found. It is an ongoing and ever-evolving conversation that includes everyone and excludes no one. Above all, it is a celebration of a long litany of courageous women who always had wisdom to share but for too long were ignored. We are all the better for Mirabai's work."

SHARON SALZBERG
author of *Real Happiness* and *Real Love*

"Mirabai Starr has untethered the sacred cow, turned on the dance music in the meditation hall, and opened the doors to let the cloisters run free! *Wild Mercy* flows through the heart of all spiritual traditions, and the heart of humanity. The women mystics in this book inspire us to listen deeply to hear the cries of the world and in our own way, with courage and commitment, respond. Mirabai so eloquently shares her soul, offering nurturance to all of us hungry for deeper meaning. This is a very important book for our time."

CELESTE YACOBONI
editor of *How Do You Pray? Inspiring Responses from Religious Leaders,
Spiritual Guides, Healers, Activists & Other Lovers of Humanity*

"Mirabai Starr. Perhaps nowhere else is her penetrating mysticism conveyed with such feminine ferocity as in her new book, *Wild Mercy*. From divine sexuality and fleshly exploitation to the sacred art of grieving, dying, and mortality salience, Mirabai takes the heart of the reader into the crevices between creation and contours, beginnings and finales, tapping the tender crescendos of living into the holy. Both powerful and compassionate, both fearless and commanding, this book is an invitation to unfold into an ampler version of the self. This is not a dispassionate read. It's an invocation of action and harbinger of complacence. This book is a must-read for every person willing to accept the decisive challenge of existence: to awaken."

JOANNE CACCIATORE, PHD
associate professor, Arizona State University, and author of *Bearing the Unbearable: Love, Loss, and the Heartbreaking Path of Grief*

"Mirabai Starr has crafted a book out of her own unique life, steeped in the outpourings of the women mystics. This is the robust, sensual, full-to-overflowing prose of one who has soaked herself in poetry and in the life-practices of those mystics: she is not "talking about"; she is reporting from the road. Be warned—to open this book is to embark upon a journey."

EVE ILSEN
singer-storyteller, psychotherapist, and rabbinic pastor

"It is by empowering the sacred feminine and by listening to the earth as she tries to communicate with us that we will ultimately heal."

LAMA TSULTRIM ALLIONE
author of *Wisdom Rising: Journey into the Mandala of the Empowered Feminine*

"Here's what will probably happen when you open this astonishing book. You will realize you are in the lap of the Great Mother and she's reading to you. Your body, habituated to the terror of being a woman in a world that disregards women, will unclench. Your worry if you are as deeply flawed as you are pretty sure you are will abate. And then Mirabai will take you a few steps further as she introduces you to a great number of soul-afire women mystics, many of which you likely haven't encountered before. Your heart, so unseen for so long, will begin to burst with pride—knowing that you are uniquely made to bring through you the very balm that the world and your fellow humans needs most. Of course, Mirabai will keep going, showing you how their wisdom can fuel your community activism, your participation in restorative justice, and your ability to tend our ailing planet Earth. The task of the divine feminine (or the divine feminist!) is not to take a wrecking ball to the patriarchal structures inside of which we all suffer. None of us can make sustainable change—whether inside us or out in the world—using the same ways of thinking (or wrecking) that created the deep hole we are trying to climb out of. This book will offer you new ways to think—and to feel, act, and commune. To read it is to drink deeply from the well of wholeness and hope. Drink, friend, drink."

LIYANA SILVER
coach, torch-holder, and author of *Feminine Genius: The Provocative Path to Waking Up and Turning On the Wisdom of Being a Woman*

"Truth and Dare. As Mirabai paints her devotional story with poetry, she gathers the flowers of various mystical traditions from around the world into a bouquet of Beauty, of connection with all aspects of ourselves, and of the interconnectedness of all beings. She gives us the essence of vast teachings and deep life explorations and motivates us to take up practical actions for manifesting this wisdom—this wisdom of the Feminine—each in our own true way."

NINA RAO
devotional musician

"In *Wild Mercy*, Mirabai Starr brings us relief like rain in a world parched by politics and angst. I found myself weeping tears of joy to come home to the sisterhood of saints and the many paths of feminine contemplative knowing that are made lovingly accessible here. Starr writes poetically and passionately, all the while toggling the spiritual opposites that trip us up, giving us teaching after teaching to free and nourish our souls. I am so grateful for *Wild Mercy*; I could not put it down."

RABBI TIRZAH FIRESTONE, PHD
author of *The Woman's Kabbalah* and *Wounds into Wisdom: Healing Intergenerational Jewish Trauma*

"It would be difficult to find a more trustworthy guide of the feminine mystics than Mirabai. In *Wild Mercy*, Mirabai's writing will lovingly pierce your consciousness, illuminating pathways that draw you far below and beyond what you thought you knew about spirituality and humanity, masculinity and femininity, and truth and grace. But even more than her beautiful writing, Mirabai's soulful guidance will lead you on a transformative cross-cultural journey as you traverse the sacred stories and wisdom of a diverse spectrum of feminine mystics. Importantly, her careful study of and sensitivity to social inequality and power dynamics enables her to highlight the deep spiritual wisdom that lies in other cultures without veering into ethnotourism. Rather, she invites readers to relinquish Western biases and entitlements as they faithfully drink from the waters that have nourished souls all over the world."

CHRISTENA CLEVELAND
associate professor, Duke Divinity School

"Mirabai Starr has gifted us over the years with lively translations of the mystics and other blessings, but with this new book she outdoes herself! *Wild Mercy* is Starr's chef d'oeuvre—in it she wrestles with one of the most important signs of hope to combat the cynicism and despair that mark our times. I speak of the rise of women and women's consciousness, and Starr goes to the source—to the great women mystics West and East—to awaken us and instruct us in what has been lacking under Patriarchy. She not only draws on mystics of the past and mystics in her storied life but also her own deep experiences of awe, of grief, of healing, of creativity, inviting us into her own personal journey. I loved her affirmation of family life as a spiritual practice—in this way and many others she dares to democratize the mystical experience by urging us to draw on our deep and sacred everyday experiences. She enlists our mysticism as an important dimension to humanity's much-needed awakening and journey to its next evolutionary stage. This book is Delicious and Dangerous and Oh-so-needed in our time! Read it. And dare to live it."

MATTHEW FOX
author of *Original Blessing, Christian Mystics,* and *The Lotus & the Rose: Conversations on Tibetan Buddhism & Mystical Christianity* with Lama Tsomo

"This is so much more than a gorgeously written book. It is an act of divine redemption, in which Mirabai Starr gives voice to every true and secret longing of the human heart. Whoever you are, whatever you thought you knew about how the Holy looks or acts, get ready to be loved into deeper reality by someone you can trust to show you the way."

BARBARA BROWN TAYLOR
New York Times bestselling author of *An Altar in the World* and *Holy Envy: Finding God in the Faith of Others*

"*Wild Mercy* is a magnificent contribution to the wave of feminine wisdom emerging into a world that has been starved of it for too long. With the kindness of a sister, the eloquence of a poet, and the authority born out of translating the text of mystical giants, Mirabai takes us by the hand, ushering us into a more immanent, devotional, and utterly human way to walk the journey home with depth and substance. May *Wild Mercy* flood our troubled world with grace."

MIRANDA MACPHERSON
author of *The Way of Grace: The Transforming Power of Ego Relaxation*

"In *Wild Mercy*, Mirabai Starr creates an eloquent invocation of the Divine Feminine. She mines the canon of women mystics to evoke the soft, mysterious embrace of the Beloved. In her own words and theirs, Mirabai takes the blazing thread of devotion and weaves a tapestry of ultimate longing. This book is her path through the thicket of existence, her way of consecrating the *lila*, the exquisite dance of illusion, and of making the jumble of human experience into One Love."

RAM DASS
author of *Be Here Now* and *Walking Each Other Home* (with Mirabai Bush)

"Mirabai Starr has already been a firmly rooted beacon shining a light into the places history might have obscured the wisdom of women. With *Wild Mercy* she seductively weaves the wisdom of the world's traditions—East, West, indigenous, and divined—as only she can, into a tapestry that takes up residence in our modern lives as inspired, healing, practical action, simultaneously comforting and fierce, as wild mercy must be: to live, love, and save the planet by. We are left knowing the truth of our own hearts' healing as the balm of salvation for the world."

REV. ANGEL KYODO WILLIAMS
Zen priest and author of *Radical Dharma:
Talking Race, Love, and Liberation*

"Mirabai embodies love, generosity, and wisdom. Her work and words compel us to be more, do better, love more fiercely, open our hearts and let the light in, and out."

MONA HAYDAR
activist, rapper, poet, chaplain

"The Great Mother is a Mystery . . . known only through surrender. Surrender only happens through Grace. Mirabai Starr leads us deep into the radiance of the many ways the Goddess reveals herself, illuminating our Path back home."

KRISHNA DAS
Kirtan master and author of *Chants of a Lifetime* and *Flow of Grace*

"I was with Mirabai the day before her daughter Jenny died. Over the years, the intense outpouring of love from her mother's heart has led Mirabai to the wild mercy she drinks in and shares from all the women mystics, poets, and teachers gathered together in this gorgeous book. With free-spirited passion, erudition, and blazing candor, Mirabai generously offers the joys, sorrows, and insights of her own fully lived life as a particularly female path to the vast universal life we share. Mirabai's writing is magic, transforming the salt of tears into the fruit of wisdom and compassion."

TRUDY GOODMAN, PHD
founding teacher at InsightLA and cofounder of the
Institute for Meditation and Psychotherapy in Boston

"I've been waiting for a book like this for a long time! *Wild Mercy* is a profound and exquisite glimpse into the wisdom, power, and love of the women mystics. The most pressing need of our time is for the wisdom of the feminine to be heard. Mirabai Starr's beautiful contribution allows everyone to hear those voices loud and clear! Highly recommended!"

MARCI SHIMOFF
#1 *New York Times* bestselling author of
Happy for No Reason and *Chicken Soup for the Woman's Soul*

"Mirabai Starr invites us to a sacred fiesta in a wild wood—my idea of a great gathering. It all feels, as she says, inexhaustibly holy. She has a deliciously rich vocabulary and mastery of language, which she spills out over the pages. Her friends, the women mystics, teach us that everything is holy—herbs, water, fire, the body, every last thing. We so need this book, our world yearning for wisdom to balance the benefits and disasters of patriarchy—in religious anzzd spiritual tradition as well as secular ones. The world will experience a rush of gratitude when this book is published."

MIRABAI BUSH
Senior Fellow, Center for Contemplative Mind in Society, and author of
Walking Each Other Home (with Ram Dass)

WILD MERCY

Also by Mirabai Starr

WILD MERCY

*Living the Fierce and Tender Wisdom
of the Women Mystics*

mirabai starr

sounds true
BOULDER, COLORADO

Sounds True
Boulder, CO 80306

Published 2019

Cover design by Jennifer Miles
Book design by Beth Skelley

Cover image by Erin Currier

Printed in Canada

Library of Congress Cataloging-in-Publication Data

Names: Starr, Mirabai, author.
Title: Wild mercy : living the fierce and tender wisdom of the women
mystics / Mirabai Starr.
Description: Boulder, CO : Sounds True, 2019.
Identifiers: LCCN 2018037735 (print) | LCCN 2018050969 (ebook) |
    ISBN 9781683643357 (ebook) | ISBN 9781683641568 (pbk.)
Subjects: LCSH: Mysticism. | Women mystics.
Classification: LCC BL625 (ebook) | LCC BL625 .S755 2019 (print) |
    DDC 204/.22082—dc23
LC record available at https://lccn.loc.gov/2018037735

10 9 8 7 6 5 4

To the loving memory of my soul sister,
Elaine Sutton, and of my soul mother,
Sri Siddhi Ma

Dance, Lalla, with nothing on
but air. Sing, Lalla,
wearing the sky.
LALLA

Contents

Prayer to the Shekinah

O Shekinah,
yours is the feminine face of the Holy,
the luminous moon who lights up the night
as we travel from captivity to liberation,
the pillar of fire who guides our way home,
the cloud hovering over the mountain peaks,
living sign that the drought is over.

You are the indwelling presence of the Divine.
Whenever we gather to praise the One
you are here in our midst.
When we cry out for justice
you make our hearts tender.
When we stand with those on the margins
you make our legs strong.
When we create works of art
and parent our children
and harvest our gardens
you guide and sustain us.

You are the Sabbath Bride, the Beloved,
returned from exile.
You restore balance in our relationships
and wholeness to our fragmented souls.
You infuse our lovemaking with honey.
You fill the cup of our hearts,
which tremble with longing,
with the wine of your answering love.
You are the song of our homecoming.

You are the Sabbath Queen, the Great Mother,
who sits at the heart of the table
tearing off hunks of the secret bread
that contains the exact flavor each of us loves best.

You feed us all,
the proud and the repentant,
the believer and the skeptic,
from your own hands.
Your unconditional forgiveness dissolves otherness.

O Shekinah,
we are the vessel for your inflowing.
Your radiance requires the clay of our embodiment.
Your flame burns at the core of the earth.
Your warmth penetrates the seedbed and animates
    the seedlings.
You bless the head of every animal
and kiss the tear-streaked face of humanity.
You are the vision that builds community,
and you are our refuge
when the fabric of community unravels.

Be with us now
as we navigate this landscape of mystery
where your most cherished attributes—
wild mercy and boundless compassion,
righteousness and wisdom—
seem to be cast aside and trampled
by imperious world powers
and we are paralyzed by helplessness.
Help us.
May we remember you and lift you up.
May we recognize your face and celebrate your beauty
in everything and everyone,
everywhere, always.
AMEN.

INTRODUCTION

opening

There is a secret fiesta going on in a wildwood, and you are invited. This party has been unfolding for millennia. Its hosts are women mystics from all branches of the soul family: Hinduism, Buddhism, Taoism, Judaism, Christianity, Islam, and every indigenous wisdom way. Its guests include anyone whose heart has ever yearned for union with the Beloved and the alleviation of suffering for all sentient beings. Which means YOU.

The gathering is secret simply because, historically, for wise women to gather openly has been to risk death. It's not that they have been afraid to die, but rather they have known in every muscle fiber that they must protect themselves because their knowledge is needed. Their love and clarity and beauty are profoundly, urgently needed. And so they have gone about in disguise, sprinkling party invitations in the public square, waiting to receive us when we come. They wait patiently, but they are excited.

Come. Feast on the mercy of Quan Yin and the compassion of Tara, the brilliance of Sophia and the shelter of the Shekinah. Break the bread of courageous prophet Mother Mary and dip it in the spicy oils of holy daughter Fatima. Drink yourself into a swoon with the songs of the ecstatic bhakti poet Mirabai and then sober up with the rigorous brilliance of Saint Teresa of Ávila. Dance your ass off with the fierce goddess Kali and her majestic sister Durga. Roll down into the boundless Valley of the Tao. Take refuge in the jewels of the Buddha-as-Woman, in the dharma as taught by women, in the sangha that gathers together a circle of wild and welcoming women.

You don't have to be female yourself to walk through these gates. Men are welcome here. You just don't get to boss us around or grab our breasts or solve our problems. You may sample our cooking and wash it down with our champagne. You may ask us to dance, and you may not pout if we decline. You may study our texts, ponder our most provocative questions. You may fall in our laps and weep if you feel the urge. We will soothe you, as we always have. And then we will send you back to the city with your pockets full of seeds to plant in the middle of it all.

The secret is out. The celebration is overflowing its banks. The joy is becoming too great to contain. The pain has grown too urgent to ignore. The earth is cracking open, and the women are rising from our hiding places and spilling onto the streets, lifting the suffering into our arms, demanding justice from the tyrants, pushing on the patriarchy and activating a paradigm shift such as the world has never seen.

Beyond Religion

Women do not always feel comfy inside traditional religious institutions. That's probably because the architecture of the world's organized religions and the furniture with which they are appointed have been designed largely by and for men. These structures are built to fit and uphold a male-dominated paradigm. Such boy-shaped arrangements no longer preclude a place at the table for women who wish to sit there, however. Across the faith traditions women are being initiated, ordained, and sanctioned as rabbis and acharyas, priests and priestesses, ministers and murshidas, lamas and shamans. We are disrupting the balance of power and reorganizing the conversation. Increasing numbers of men, secure in their positions of privilege and authority, are voluntarily abdicating their power and handing it over to women, calling God "she" from the pulpit, seeding the academy with female philosophers. The alienation of the feminine is as obvious to them—and as perilous—as it is to the women who have been historically excluded from positions of leadership.

Many of us, however, are not even interested in being invited to join the fraternity. It's not a matter of wanting to storm the gates of the male-dominated religions and take back what we consider to be rightfully ours. We have no desire to wear the mantle of the king. We'd rather take off all such coverings and go about naked. Replace the crown of jewels with a crown of daisies. Praise one another's beauty and wisdom and build fires to keep one another warm. We would much rather be undefined than ordained in traditions that don't fit our curves.

This does not mean that we see religion as a waste of time. Far from it! What we see is that the world's great wisdom traditions are like a giant garden of the spirit, every flower and weed, each tree and species of blooming grass a unique and glorious example of the Beloved's beauty. Like bees, we draw nectar from them all. We cross-pollinate, helping to propagate and support a more robust and resilient ecosphere. And, like bees, we are fully capable of discerning between life-giving nectar and noxious dreck. We know better than to drink the poison. Teachings of love and compassion: nectar. Messages that otherize and extol violence: toxic. We gather what is best and take it back to the Queen Bee, the Source, who transforms it into honey, a sweet and golden substance with which we nourish ourselves and feed the world.

While many of us feel suspicious of religious hierarchy and alienated by religious dogma, we are deeply drawn to the essence of the world's wisdom ways, and we find tastes of that elixir in the teachings of the mystics—especially the women mystics—of every spiritual tradition. If you are a woman who has been turned off by the established religious institutions but light up in the face of the ecstatic poetry of Mechthild of Magdeburg or Rabia of Basra, if you feel moved to nurture a personal relationship with Quan Yin or Kali, this book may be for you. If your heart is as likely to open at the feet of White Buffalo Calf Woman as at those of Our Lady of Guadalupe and you find wisdom in the teachings of the Qur'an as well as the Tao Te Ching, this journey in the footsteps of the women mystics across (and beyond) the landscape of the world's spiritual traditions is likely your journey.

My Surprise

I should probably tell you how I got this way. How I came to bow at the altars of so many different holy houses—all of them, really—and how it is I came to write this book.

First I will tell you what didn't happen. I didn't start off safely ensconced in a single religion from which I was eventually compelled to make my getaway. I am not a refugee from my ancestral Judaism, nor am I a recovering Catholic. My family was not evangelical, and I did not fall into the clutches of a cult. I was never ever taught to believe that one religion had all the answers and that the others were wrong (or worse, evil). No one ever told me I'd burn in hell for practicing yoga or chanting the Ninety-nine Names of Allah.

Rather, I was raised in the counterculture of the 1970s in a community that appreciated the wisdom of multiple spiritual paths, even as it rejected the divisive dogmas obscuring these treasures. I grew up exposed to all of the major branches of Buddhism, from the windswept emptiness of Japanese Zen to the lush layers of Vajrayana, Buddhism's tantric path. In our family we honored Jesus as a great rabbi and consulted the I Ching, the Chinese book of divination, when we had to make important decisions. At any given time there might be a sadhu, a wandering holy man, from India at our kitchen table, sitting beside an indigenous elder from the Taos Pueblo of New Mexico. This was normal.

I was drawn to every single flavor of spirit food. Curiosity developed into passion and was seasoned with study. I encountered, embraced, and assimilated many of the world's great religions and found that I could comfortably accommodate them without them crashing into one another and waging war inside of me. I was shocked to discover when I set out into the world that not everybody was one of each. My adult life has been a matter of coming to grips with this troubling fact and doing what I can to mitigate it.

Men Are Not the Bad Guys

Because the balance of masculine and feminine has been so terribly out of whack in human history, it may be tempting for women to blame everything from sexual exploitation in the workplace to the looming climate catastrophe on men and to project our rage onto all members of the male half of the species. I am endeavoring to avoid this snare. Indigenous wisdom, modern psychology, and the lived experience of most humans have demonstrated that we all contain both feminine and masculine elements in our psyches, and they vary in degree at different phases of our lives and in response to changing conditions.

I see gender much the same way as I view religion. As humanity evolves, many of us locate ourselves on an ever-flowing gender spectrum—as women who lead with certain masculine impulses, for instance, and men whose feminine sensibilities are pronounced. The contemporary interspiritual movement, too, is a natural response to a range of human expressions of the sacred. Confining ourselves to a binary gender identity (individuals who claim to be either male or female) or an exclusive religious tribe (Christianity, Buddhism, Wicca) no longer feels valid to many of us.

And yet there are jewels in each of the world's great spiritual traditions that are worthy of safekeeping. Similarly, there is a healing elixir in the feminine experience that has been historically relegated to the fringes and that I believe the human family is ready to reclaim at last. With its emphasis on the value of relationships, feelings, and mutual empowerment over individual success and empirical argument, I believe in the healing energy of the feminine as a fire that can melt the frozen heart of the world, the artistry that will mend the tattered web of interconnection.

Tapestry

Here's how I have built this book: Each chapter of *Wild Mercy* is a tapestry of my favorite teachings from women of wisdom of the past and present, interwoven with my own reflections and personal stories and ending with a suggested practice—often, but not always, a writing prompt—so that you can integrate the topic at hand with your own experience. Because of my love for haiku, I open each chapter with a three-line poem, crafted in the traditional five-seven-five-syllable structure, to serve as a distilled essence of that theme. Each chapter focuses on a particular station of the women's wisdom journey, such as navigating heartbreak or walking the path of creative self-expression. To illumine each topic, I have selected certain mystics, goddesses, contemporary teachers, and seekers from a vast array of possible exemplars. I could easily have included dozens of others and have allowed my particular intimacy with each one to guide many of my choices.

It is my hope that you, like I, will find yourself shining from the luminous mirror of these wisdom beings. That you will identify with their struggles and be encouraged by their breakthroughs. That you will forge living relationships with them as your ancestors and guides, draw on their power, embody their essential qualities. It is my prayer that together we will welcome the wisdom of women back into the collective field, where it may help to transform the human family and heal the ravaged earth.

This book is more than a book. It is an invitation. We are making a flying carpet here to carry us through our lives as contemporary mystics masquerading as ordinary people—people who hear the call both to turn inward and to step up, to cultivate a contemplative life and to offer the fruits in service. Thanks to an array of wise and wild women and a few goddesses, the way is flooded in light, even—perhaps especially—when our eyes perceive it as dark.

Enter the garden
Where walls melt and trees blossom
Vibrant quietude

TURNING INWARD

Cultivating Contemplative Life

opening

Contemplative life flows in a circular pattern: awe
provokes introspection, which invokes awe.

Maybe you're making dinner and you step outside
to snip chives from the kitchen garden just as the
harvest moon is rising over the eastern slopes. She is
full and golden, like one of those pregnant women who
radiate from within. Suddenly you cannot bear the
beauty. Scissors suspended in your hand, tears pooling
at the corners of your eyes, you nearly quit breathing.
Your gaze softens, and the edges of your individual
identity fade. You are absorbed into the heart of the
moon. It feels natural, and there is no other place you'd
rather be. But the onions are burning, and so you
turn away and cut your herbs and go back inside. You
resume stirring the sauce and setting the table.

This is not the first time you have disappeared
into something beautiful. You have experienced the
unfettering of the subject-object distinction while
holding your daughter's hand as she labored to give
birth to your grandson; when you curled up in bed

with your dying friend and sang her Haskiveinu, the Hebrew prayer for a peaceful sleep; while yielding to your lover's lips. You have lost yourself in heartbreak, then lost the desire to ever regain yourself, then lost your fear of death. You long ago relinquished your need for cosmic order and personal control. You welcome unknowingness.

Which is why seemingly ordinary moments like moonrises and lovemaking undo you. The veil has been pulled back. Everything feels inexhaustibly holy. This is not what they taught you in the church of your childhood. Your soul has been formed in the forge of life's losses, galvanized in the crucible of community, fertilized by the rain of relationship, blessed by your intimacy with Mother Earth. You have glimpsed the face of the Divine where you least expected it.

And this is why you cultivate contemplative practice. The more you intentionally turn inward, the more available the sacred becomes. When you sit in silence and turn your gaze toward the Holy Mystery you once called God, the Mystery follows you back out into the world. When you walk with a purposeful focus on breath and birdsong, your breathing and the twitter of the chickadee reveal themselves as a miracle. When you eat your burrito mindfully, gratitude for every step that led to the perfect combination of beans and cheese and tortilla—from grain and sunlight to rain and migrant labor—fills your heart and renders you even more inclined to be grateful.

So you sit down to meditate not only because it helps you to find rest in the arms of the formless Beloved but also because it increases your chances of being stunned by beauty when you get back up. Encounters with the sacred that radiate from the core of the ordinary embolden you to cultivate stillness and simple awareness. In the midst of a world that is begging you to distract yourself, this is no easy practice. Yet you keep showing up. You are indomitable. You are thirsty for wonder.

The Magic Carpet of Practice

For women mystics, contemplative life is not so much a matter of transcending the illusions of mundane existence or attaining states of perfect equanimity as it is about becoming as fully present as possible to the realities of the human experience. In showing up for *what is*, no matter how pedestrian or tedious, how aggravating or shameful, the *what is* begins to reveal itself as imbued with holiness. How do we make space in our lives for this kind of sacred seeing?

It doesn't hurt to engage in some kind of disciplined practice, such as meditation or prayer. Silent sitting becomes a magic carpet that rescues us from identifying with every neurotic thought that pops into our minds and every emotional distraction that threatens to abduct us. When we purposely build periods of reverence or stillness into our days, we practice gazing through the eyes of love, and we get better and better at seeing love everywhere we look. Your practice may take the shape of twenty minutes a day on a cushion or aimless solitary walks on the beach. It can look like kneeling in a church or a mosque or simply like following the flow of one breath to the next with your full attention.

FROM ALTERED STATES TO DESERT MIND

It took me a couple of decades of meditation practice to make my way home to the feminine contemplative path. I began my quest at fourteen. My initial training was framed by a masculine approach: it was all about crushing the ego and distrusting the body. My goal was to detach from the material plane and travel in the astral realms, an approach that aligned with my adolescent craving for transcendent modes. I was a dramatic teenager (you might have been, too). By the time I began formally studying and practicing meditative methods, not only had my life already been marked by multiple significant deaths, including the passings of my older brother and my first boyfriend, but I was having spontaneous experiences of altered states of consciousness (most likely triggered by an accidental dose of LSD at a party when I was thirteen) that knocked me off my feet and left me breathless and terrified.

I dealt with the drama through poetry. I read it. I wrote it. I composed simple melodies in a minor key and sang my poems to myself beside the Hondo River, nestled among the red willows near my home in Taos, New Mexico, and made myself cry. I drew abstract self-portraits in profile in a blank artist's book, depicting myself with enormous sad eyes, presumably evidence of deep wisdom. I was the perfect candidate for spiritual trickery.

Along came a charlatan master who convinced me that my terrifying dissociative states were evidence of my impending enlightenment and that all I needed was someone to cultivate my sainthood and that (surprise!) he was just the man for the job. He encouraged me to leave home and move to the commune in the mountains where he lived so that he could orchestrate my awakening. Although I was not yet fifteen, my parents agreed to this arrangement. It was the 1970s, the height of the counterculture movement, and conventional social structures like the nuclear family were being reevaluated. Besides, I was on fire with desire for God, and my parents (distracted by fires of their own) trusted me.

My teacher would wake me in my freezing A-frame at 3 a.m. ("the hour of the saints and masters," he explained) and escort me to a small adobe cell to engage in rigorous yogic breathing practices that temporarily paralyzed me, and then he would wrap me in a blanket and hold me while I returned to my body, trembling.

I meditated. I meditated in the mornings before school and in the evenings before dinner. I meditated when I lay down to sleep and when I woke in the night. I had visions. I saw colors and heard weird music and remembered past lives. I pierced the veil of maya, rendering everything I could experience through my senses as illusory. And then I let my teacher have sex with me, because, according to him, that was a crucial element of my liberation and therefore of the liberation of all sentient beings.

As you can see, there were a few things about all this that were very wrong. The most obvious one is the sexual abuse, and I have spent much of my adult life healing from this violation and trying to support women and girls in reclaiming the sovereignty of their own bodies. But what I really want to talk about here is that at the same time as I was brainwashed into giving my body away to a man who had no right to it, I was being conditioned to see the body as an illusion to be risen above. Meditation was the ticket to this blessed transcendence. By assuming a certain posture and closing my eyes, by employing mantras and visualizations, I set out on the open road of consciousness, stuck out my spiritual thumb, and hitched a ride to the edges of the cosmos. I broke through into planes of consciousness where I faced up to whatever supernatural shenanigans awaited me, leaving my pesky little body in the dust. This, I thought, was what it meant to be spiritual.

Healing from my exploitation involved not only escaping the charlatan master but salvaging the sanctity of my body and inching my way toward a more female-positive approach to things. This reclamation project spilled into my spiritual life and permeated the interior landscape. I began to leave the altered states behind, trade the razzle-dazzle of paranormal phenomena for the blessing of *the ordinary*. I flirted with the possibility of fully inhabiting the present moment, willing to investigate things as they are and myself as I am. I started looking with curiosity and kindness. As I developed this method of mindfulness, the impulse to be present expanded beyond the cushion and into the open field of my life. I had moments of glimpsing all phenomena with a fearless and compassionate gaze: my very own dirty kitchen and the corruption in politics, changing a diaper and changing a tire, making love and making airline reservations. These moments have grown more consistent over decades of practice.

I don't blame my adolescent girl self for falling for the illusion that the spiritual life is about transcending the body and thereby leaving my body vulnerable to exploitation. She was on the right track—hungry for truth, thirsty for the love that is as big as the universe, ready for anything. She was brave and she was wise. But she confused the fireworks for the sun.

Eventually, I needed to make my way to the desert and sit down there. Sit quietly all night and then sit still all day until the landscape revealed itself as not barren at all but rather teeming with life. (Don't we all? Doesn't everyone sometimes need to hang out in blessed unknowing?)

We do not need to be afraid of the emptiness. It is in boundlessness that we meet the Real and recognize it as the face of Love. It is in groundlessness that we find our way home. When religious ideologies and their associated spiritual practices begin to take us away from our lives instead of connecting us with the center of ourselves, we need to be willing to let them go. To not be in a hurry to replace them. Instead, we can shift our focus back to the ordinary and bless it with the gift of our full attention. Then watch in awe as it brims with holy light.

NONDUALITY AND DEVOTION

Perhaps you, like I, have associated spirituality with rising above the human condition, rather than with consciously embodying it. We've set mind against body, elevated abstraction over engagement. We buy into a belief system that bullies us into affirming our essential coidentity with the Divine, even when we do not subjectively experience it.

Isn't it peculiar how many of us on a contemporary spiritual path have stumbled into the trap that sets up devotion and nondualism as mutually exclusive? Nondualists have grown rigidly dualistic in this regard! We deem the devotional impulse to be delusion and set up absolute consciousness as exclusively true.

If I've left you in the dust here, let me catch you up with some working definitions. *Nondualism*, also known as *nonduality*, is the belief (yes, *belief*, as opposed to *fact*) that Ultimate Reality is undivided, "not two." Notice that it does not assert that all is one but simply acknowledges that in a state of awakened consciousness all subject-object distinctions do not exist. They are transcended. There is no "I" as opposed to "other." Any concept of ourselves as separate from God dissolves in the open sky of pure awareness. This is very nice, but why do nondualists have to also dis the devoted?

The prejudice I keep encountering—especially among what I would characterize as the Neo–Advaita Vedanta crowd, and which I'm attempting to expose here—goes like this: Nondual consciousness is superior to the devotional experience because devotion implies a naïve belief in the separation from the object of our longing (God; Love). Nondualism gets the cosmic joke and knows that it's impossible to be separate from the one we love because there is only one Ultimate Reality and we are part of it. Therefore, devotion is an immature inclination that is born of sublimated emotional impulses. But nondualism is a sign of spiritual maturity and should be the goal of all spiritual practice (without being goal oriented, of course, which would be dualistic).

This argument is not fair. And it is not feminine. By that I mean that if the feminine is all about incarnation and embodiment (which is what I am proclaiming in this book), then she rests squarely in the realm of form. And in form we have separation as well as unity. We have mountain ranges and blue spruces, inner cities and dive bars, old white dudes and radical black feminists. We have teenagers in prison and moms who pine for them, grieving widows and philandering husbands, people for whom meditation practice compels them to offer themselves in service to those on the margins and other people who don't give a shit. This world is filled with glorious, untidy multiplicity. Sometimes God feels very far away, and so we long for God. Not because we believe that God and self are ultimately existentially separate, but because here in the midst of our relative reality our souls yearn to return to where we come from: Absolute Love.

So when we engage in devotional practices like chanting the names of the Divine in any of the world's great sacred languages or making offerings to Christ or Krishna or Quan Yin, we are opening our hearts, and our hearts are boundless. That's where we awaken to the essential truth of not twoness. This is not an -ism; it's a lived reality, germinated in the rich, dark soil of our devotional, form-filled experience. Rather than serve as an obstacle to undifferentiated consciousness, devotion becomes the path to what the great feminine mystic Julian of Norwich called "oneing." A position of twoness (our little selves pining for the Divine) becomes the springboard into the infinite land-scape of not twoness. And this experience of unity with the All (which is, by its nature, usually fleeting) fills our hearts and compels us to devote ourselves all over again.

I have never experienced the sublime quiet of formlessness as being at odds with my longing for and praise of God. To my mind, we are vast enough beings to synthesize these seemingly opposite attributes into a robust and animated third truth. We do not require adherence to any particular dogma—even those that seem especially enlightened—to guide our way home to the Divine. Most of the mystics I adore have had a similar hybrid of devotional and nondual experiences and outlooks. Maybe you are this breed of seeker. Let us engage, and even invent, practices that feel aligned with our own spiritual sensibilities.

Trusting our soul's innate knowingness, flinging ourselves into the mystery. Practicing in multiple spaces, with diverse communities and alone, allowing your edges to melt into the One. Then letting your heart break open all over again when you remember the unbearable beauty of the Beloved's invisible face.

Teresa of Ávila

The important thing is not to think much,
but to love much, and so to do whatever best
awakens you to love.   TERESA OF ÁVILA

I like to believe that we are all encircled by an invisible ring of loving ancestors, made up of our mothers and grandmothers and great-grandmothers, plus women of wisdom no longer living whom we honor as mentors, whether or not we ever met them in the flesh. I also sense there the presence of the goddesses whose stories guide our steps, along with countless unseen beings we may never even know are here with us. Let me acquaint you with the one I consider to be my personal "matron saint": Teresa of Ávila. Investigate her masterworks (which I have had the privilege of translating into contemporary, accessible English), such as *The Interior Castle* and *The Book of My Life*, and see if she takes up residence in your own inner sanctuary, too.

Teresa is a luminous example of a devotional nature that conjoins with the lived experience of nondual states. Born into the turbulent epoch of the Spanish Inquisition, Teresa was a first-generation *conversa* from a Jewish family that had the good fortune to be able to buy their way out of exile and the gumption to go through the motions of converting to Christianity. But when Teresa's father was a boy, his own father was accused of secretly practicing his ancestral Jewish traditions, which resulted in his family being publicly shamed. Actually, since Jewish rituals are mostly observed in the home and presided over by the women, it would most likely have been Teresa's grandmother who had been doing the practicing. Perhaps she dared to light the Sabbath candles and welcome the Sabbath Bride, the spirit of Shabbat, and then bless the children. Yet the whole family took the heat. They were dragged from their house and paraded around the streets of Toledo for seven Fridays in a row, forced to kneel at every Catholic shrine in the city while church officials denounced them and ordinary citizens spat at them and hurled anti-Semitic curses.

Teresa's father was determined that his own children would never endure the humiliation he suffered. He turned his back on Judaism and fostered a devout Catholic household. By the time Teresa was born in 1515, the only flavor of religious experience available to her, both in the Spanish culture at large and in her own traumatized family, was Christianity, and to speak of any other option was to risk banishment or death. But it had only been a few years since the great expulsion of Jews and Muslims in 1492, and so the fragrance of Judaism and Islam lingered in the air every Spanish Catholic breathed. That's likely why Teresa's prose is peppered with the Jewish impulse to argue with everything, especially God. And why the poetry of her protégé, John of the Cross, is steeped in images of gardens and wine, which we find everywhere in Sufism, the mystical branch of Islam.

Teresa grew up with an ambivalent relationship with the church. She loved Christ but was wary of Christianity. Whether or not she was conscious of her own Jewish roots and the very real danger these posed, she seems to have perceived the heavy hand of the institutionalized church as an impediment to her lived experience of faith. Why, Teresa must have wondered, must intimacy with the Beloved be relegated to second place behind corporate loyalty? Even as she declared herself a faithful daughter of the church until the day she died, the spiritual vacuity of some of its customs left Teresa cold.

When she was twelve, her thirty-three-year-old mother died in childbirth with her ninth child, and Teresa turned to Mother Mary. She nurtured this relationship with the Blessed Mother throughout her life, but this connection did not magically subdue the girl or render her meek and mild. By the time she was sixteen, Teresa was constantly getting into trouble. At last, she became embroiled in a scandal dramatic enough that her father sent her away to a convent to be "educated" (i.e., *controlled*). In her writings Teresa never specifies what transgression she committed. Did she lose her virginity? Did she take an unchaperoned walk in the garden with a boy? Was she caught kissing a girl? All we know is that by banishing her to the nunnery, Teresa's father was wagering that his wayward daughter would chill out and learn some womanly skills before returning home to commence a respectable life, marrying an appropriate gentleman and making babies.

Accustomed to an unusual degree of freedom in her motherless household, at first Teresa pushed back against the rules and restrictions of religious life. Naturally gregarious and talkative, she felt stifled by the imposed silence and solitude. Little by little, however, her psyche seemed to settle and her nervous system to relax. She began to take refuge in the daily sessions of contemplative prayer, finding a secret oasis in the quiet spaciousness between periods of vocal liturgy.

So it was a different kind of subversive act, another act of rebellion altogether, when Teresa informed her father that she wished to actually join the convent to which she had been exiled and profess her vows as a nun. Her long-suffering dad did not see this coming. He tried to talk her out of it. It was obvious to everyone who knew her—to Teresa, most of all—that this was not a girl suited to monastic life. Indeed, Teresa spent the next twenty years languishing in self-imposed isolation from the world she loved. She could not accommodate herself to a small and regimented reality. And so finally, after a couple of decades, she created a new one. From the inside.

But first she had to experience a radical conversion of the heart.

OPENING THE FLOODGATES

It wasn't until Teresa was in her late thirties that she stumbled upon her Beloved at last and fell headlong into a love affair that would transfigure her life. One day, as she was striding through the convent hallway, she noticed a statue of Christ scourged at the pillar, bound and crowned with thorns. In preparation for an upcoming celebration, someone had left it leaning against the wall. Annoyed, Teresa bent to pick it up and carry it to an appropriate location. This is when her glance caught the gaze of the suffering Christ, and their eyes locked.

His countenance undid her—the blend of harrowing pain and unconditional love, of vulnerability and intimacy. Teresa's heart filled and flooded, releasing her from her exile in the religious desert and catapulting her into the garden of mystical connection. She flung herself onto the stone floor in full prostration and, unleashing tears she had contained all her life, apologized to her Beloved for having neglected him, promising always to remember this great love. In fact, true to her defiant nature, Teresa refused to get up until he could assure her that he would never let her forget how deeply she loved him. Christ heeded Teresa's demands. Their love was a flame that animated her till the day she died, an ever-flowing cup of wine that continually intoxicated her.

This "second conversion" of Teresa's in the convent hallway triggered her propensity for experiencing ecstatic states. But this tendency toward rapture was balanced by her desire to be of service. She wanted everyone—especially women—to have access to direct connection with the Divine inside the sanctuary of their own souls. She founded a reform movement called the Barefoot (Discalced) Carmelites, in honor of her commitment to the contemplative values of voluntary simplicity, solitary quietude, and intimacy with the Beloved in unceasing prayer.

When Teresa was fifty-two, she encountered the brilliant young mystic who would come to be known as John of the Cross, another member of the devotional/nondual hybrid tribe I have been describing. With characteristic charm and eloquence, Teresa persuaded John to partner with her in founding contemplative communities all over Spain. The pair was persecuted for their efforts. When John was twenty-nine, a group of mitigated (mainstream) Carmelite brothers broke into his room in the middle of the night and abducted him. They carried him to a remote monastery in the hills outside Toledo and locked him in a tiny, fetid cell that had once been a latrine, where he languished for nine months.

John's horrific incarceration became the catalyst for his spiritual descent into the depths of darkness that paradoxically delivered him to a wellspring of light. From this unexpected luminescence he drank deeply. With nowhere to hide from the pain of betrayal by his own brethren, and feeling abandoned by the God he loved, John gradually transformed. His inner reality became a state of spiritual nakedness, and there he experienced union with the Beloved, the object of his heart's deepest longing. This transformation gave rise to the teachings for which John of the Cross is famous, what he called "the dark night of the soul," as well as to his ecstatic poetry.

Meanwhile, Teresa plunged into a period of unrelenting visions, voices, and raptures, which often unfolded in public settings, such as the convent chapel during Mass, in which she occasionally levitated! These dramatic episodes caught the attention of the Spanish Inquisition; coupled with the impurity of her blood, tainted by her family's recent Jewishness, this was all the excuse they needed to investigate her. They demanded that the middle-aged nun document every spiritual incident she had ever experienced, as far back as she could remember, so that they could determine whether this pattern indicated delusion caused by the devil or supported her claims of being blessed by the Divine. If they could prove that Teresa had been captured by the spirit of evil, they could justify shutting down the reform she led. But Teresa so charmed the inquisitors with her wit and insight that they ended up blessing her dissident project in spite of themselves.

NOT TWO

I see John and Teresa as a kind of Möbius strip, each one curving to complete the other. While they both exemplify this dual/nondual love dance, their personalities led them to express it differently, and their genders seem to have reinforced their distinct experiences. John's outward demeanor was characterized by reticence, quietude, invisibility. Inwardly, John was on fire with passionate yearning for union with the Beloved, intent on escaping from concepts and the house of the senses to meet up with the Beloved for a secret rendezvous in the garden. Outwardly, Teresa was dramatic, emotional, extroverted. But her inner life was bathed in the sweet peace of companionship with the One she loved.

Let's say that Teresa's way is the way of the feminine. She fully inhabited and embodied her life. For Teresa, merging with God meant turning inward and following the fragrance of love all the way to the center of her own being, where the Beloved dwelled. It's from here that he called to her and from here he welcomed her home. She found traces of this presence everywhere she went. This is the trajectory Teresa so masterfully describes in her guide to spiritual development, *The Interior Castle*. Her spirituality is Christ-centric. Jesus is the form that connects Teresa to the formless. The space where she meets her God is intimate, womb-like, and profoundly personal. The convention among the Spanish mystics of referring to God as the masculine Beloved (He) and the soul as the feminine lover (she) reflects the earthy eroticism of this relationship.

As we have seen, most of the world's great religions have tended to emphasize transcending the body and other mundane distractions. This is no surprise, since their primary administrators have historically been men determined to conquer their bodily attachments to be worthy of the Divine encounter. Meanwhile, back in the kitchen, it is the women who transmit the living heart of religion, lighting the candles, singing the prayers, cleaning up the afterbirth, and bathing the dead. "God," Teresa famously declared, "lives among the pots and pans."

Like a favorite aunt discovered in adulthood, Teresa has become my "shero," my confidante, my role model for living a passionately engaged life in which the lines between immanence and transcendence disappear and contemplation and action are inseparable. But I did not always recognize Teresa of Ávila as my ally. In fact, when I first encountered her I tried to sidestep her. She appeared to be standing between me and my love interest, Saint John of the Cross, whose quiet radiance I have always adored. For John, union was a matter of "climbing a secret ladder in disguise" up and out of this relative world to a place where "all my senses were suspended," as he declares in his own masterwork, *Dark Night of the Soul.*

But then there was Teresa, overshadowing him with her flashy fire. While John, in characteristically masculine fashion, slipped into his solitary cave in the hills above the monastery in Segovia to meditate on La Nada (Holy Emptiness), Teresa charged across the Castilian countryside, founding convents and subverting authority. For John, union with God was about dismantling, disassembling, deconstructing all corporeal and conceptual forms in a passionate pursuit of the Formlessness that lies beyond the realm of the senses and intellect. For Teresa, union was a matter of embracing every particle of inescapable reality as imbued with, dripping with, overflowing with divinity.

I used to think these perspectives on the Holy One were mutually exclusive. John's desert spirituality. Teresa's earthy warmth. But as it turns out, they are identical. John's practice of resting in the emptiness sparked his blaze of adoration. His passion for God is unmatched in the literary canon of any religion in any age. Teresa's impulse to pray and praise yielded her to a state of blessed nonduality. For her, the highest form of prayer was what she called "The Prayer of Quiet," in which the soul simply rests in the presence of the Friend and any trace of separation between them evaporates. Once I recognized that both of these approaches—the dual and the nondual, the devotional and the ascetic—abide comfortably together in my own soul, any meaningful discrepancy between these two Spanish mystics dissolved.

In the terms of devotion, the lover (the soul) and Beloved (the Divine) begin as one. The lover suffers from the illusion of separation, but then lover and Beloved are restored to oneness. The soul's longing leads to divine union. In the terms of nonduality, the lover and Beloved have never been two; they have always been one and ever shall be. The soul's task is simply to *remember*.

Finding Our Inner Queendom

Teresa of Ávila's theology of innerness was revolutionary. She saw that the soul of every human being is designed as a kind of queendom—a magnificent "interior castle"—with softly rounded rooms leading ever inward toward a luminous center inhabited by Love itself. It is a blessed realm meant for all of us. Teresa of Ávila extends a radical invitation to drop our moralistic self-recriminations, dispense with dogma, strip off the cloak of our preconceptions, and step naked into the arms of the Beloved. The intimacy we discover there inspires us to harvest the fruits of love and feed the hungry world.

In her vision of the soul as an interior castle, Teresa identifies seven stations of the journey to divine union, using the analogy of seven primary dwellings within the palace. The outer spaces represent the beginning of our journey home. The light of the Divine is dim at first, and her voice is faint. But both the radiance and the God song increase in clarity and volume the closer we come to the center.

The early stations are concerned with discipline and humility. Here we intentionally cultivate self-knowledge. We engage in contemplative prayer as a way to be closer to the Beloved.

We may not always see her or feel her in the dark. It's like sleeping next to someone at night, Teresa tells us. You don't need visual or tactile evidence to know she is there. In fact, it would be crazy to believe she is gone just because you don't see her. Listen for the sound of her breath. Take comfort in her proximity.

As the journey unfolds it builds momentum. We have met the one we love. We have fallen head over heels. Our love has been reciprocated. The wedding date is set. Now we cannot wait to consummate. We defy convention and take the most direct path to union, even if that route does not appear on any map. Who has patience for maps? We dispense with all suggestions and plunge into the wild. We turn inward.

Contemplative life is a tapestry of intention and surrender, of reaching out and letting go, of stillness and exhilaration, form and formlessness. It is devotional *and* nondual. It is grounded in our connection with the Earth and our interconnectedness with all beings. *And* it is about moments of rapture in the face of the most ordinary phenomena, in which our particular embodied experience gives way to an undifferentiated melding with All That Is. This is the dance of masculine and feminine, which call each other from the core of our soul DNA, demanding reunification and wholeness.

GARDEN OF PRAYER

Teresa compares developing contemplative life to cultivating a garden. In her *Vida* (*Life Story*), she thrills herself by coming up with the analogy of "four waters of prayer." The first water of prayer is labor-intensive. We walk to the well, lower a bucket down, down, down, and then haul it up. Water sloshes over the sides, and we lose about half. Then we have to schlep it across the yard to the garden, where we carefully pour it on the ground and beg the seeds to germinate. This equates to intentionally nurturing a discipline of contemplative practice.

The second water of prayer still requires effort, but there is some support. We crank a waterwheel, which draws the water from the source and channels it along an elaborately engineered aqueduct, delivering the water through a spout into a waiting vessel some distance away. The water splashes noisily and makes a big deal of itself as it arrives. We keep meditating. We have moments of insight.

The third water of prayer is more direct. Through an arrangement of irrigation ditches (a system designed by the Moors of medieval Spain), we simply lift a wooden gate and the water flows from the *acequia madre*, the "mother ditch," along each channel, nourishing the tender shoots by soaking the ground around them. We rest in deepening states of quiet.

The fourth and by far most efficacious water of prayer is rain. And rain is grace. It can be neither forced nor engineered, neither cajoled nor bargained for. Rain is a gift from Spirit. Our only task is to receive it and lift our hands in praise. Our individual identity softens, and we remember we are already one with the One, and always have been, and ever shall be.

Spiritual Warriors

Contemplative life is not for the timid. It's scary to be quiet, and it takes courage to be still. No one could be expected to sit on the battlefield of her own mind without being armed with the sword of unconditional truth in one hand and the sword of unconditional love in the other. And yet neither is the journey inward a journey for the elite. It is not necessary to pass through elaborate initiations and pay for expensive seminars to earn access to a place where we can meet Reality and say yes to it. When we turn inward, investigating the present moment with patience and inquisitiveness, we become a beach across which the wave of love may break and transform the topography of our soul. My friend Miranda Macpherson calls this inflowing experience "nectar," invoking both its sweetness and its nourishing quality.

Miranda had a spontaneous awakening while sitting in the cave of the twentieth century's great teacher of Advaita Vedanta (nondualism) Ramana Maharshi (1879–1950) in India. At that point, she had already spent years leading groups in contemplative practices. She was a spiritual director directing other spiritual directors. Her specialty was interspiritual devotional practices, such as guided visualizations and chanting, and she drew on wisdom teachings from all the world's great traditions. The core element of Miranda's approach was prayer (devotion), and the various methods of praising the One filled her heart and affected her students in a similarly uplifting way. It was hard to avoid getting hooked on these sweet encounters with the reality of love.

But the reliably overflowing spirit vessel emptied out that day in the cave. Miranda heard Ramana's voice (though he had left his body decades earlier). "Be still," he said. "Be nothing. Do nothing. Get nothing. Become nothing. Relinquish nothing. Rest in God." In that moment, without hesitation, Miranda surrendered. She released the rich content of her spiritual life and let go of the sublime teachings she had studied. As she stepped into the nondual void, all those years of meditating and praying, of chanting and visualizing, fell away, and Miranda plunged into the heart of the mystery. This unsettling descent into spiritual and conceptual groundlessness continued to unfold for many months, and her former life unraveled with it. She left the center she had founded in London and entered a period of relative seclusion in California.

Then, one day while Miranda was running in the woods, a Hindu chant bubbled up from the ground of her being and emerged in song: *Sri Ram Jai Ram Jai Jai Ram Om.* This flow of sacred song took Miranda by surprise. She had not sung devotional music in many months. She had become incapable of engaging in the dualistic practices that had formerly been so central to her life. But now the love energy was flowing freely into the hollowed-out space of her soul.

"My heart felt as if it just exploded with light and love and ecstatic praise," Miranda told me. "In that moment I realized that it was *That* praising *That* in my heart. As the Sufis say, 'It is the Beloved's own love that loves the Beloved in me.' This was the day that prayer, devotion, and chanting returned to my life, but not as a method to get anywhere." Rather, Miranda describes this upwelling of adoration as a natural recirculation of that nectar of grace, which is our true nature.

When we sing sacred music, we sit beneath a rushing fountain of love that washes over us and leaves us in a state of holy hush. Ecstasy empties into stillness. The Holy praises herself and grows silent. Into that silence we may fall and fall forever.

Gate Gate Paragate Parasamgate Bodhi Svaha! This is the great Buddhist blessing at the end of the Heart Sutra, known as the Prajnaparamita (which is the embodiment of the Divine Feminine, by the way). "Gone, gone, gone beyond, gone beyond the beyond. All hail to the one who goes!"

deepening

To cultivate contemplative life, I suggest making a commitment to a daily sitting practice for thirty days. If you have a regular practice now or have sustained one in the past, try a new method and see if it revitalizes your contemplative experience. If you are new to meditation, I encourage you to investigate some of the traditional techniques listed below. It's best to learn these methods under the guidance of a teacher or experienced practitioner. Yet even just ten to twenty minutes of following the arc of your inhale and exhale while in a seated posture, with eyes closed or softly gazing downward, can change your life.

Notice, as you experiment, whether you are naturally drawn to devotional practices or to a practice of total absorption. Where does your heart feel most happy? Or is it happy in both? Try various methods, including (but not limited to):

- Mindfulness (secular)
- Vipassana, or insight meditation
- Metta, or loving-kindness
- Tonglen, or "sending and taking"
- Zazen
- Centering Prayer
- Lectio Divina, or secular reading
- Mantra
- Dhikr, or repetition of divine names
- Visualization

Keep a daily journal of your experiences to track your journey.

Indwelling lover
Bread, wine, candlelight
Everything belongs

LAYING DOWN OUR BURDEN

Keep the Sabbath Holy

opening

Here. Come here. Take a moment to set aside that list
you've been writing in fluorescent ink. The list that converts
tasks into emergencies. Items like "feed the orchids" become
"If I don't accomplish this by 11:00 a.m. tomorrow morning
the rain forests are going to dry up and it will be all my
fault." Or "If I fail to renew my automobile insurance I will
probably crash my car and everyone will die." Or "This
friend just had her breast biopsied and that friend's brother-
in-law beat up her sister and my aunt just lost her job with
the symphony and my nephew is contemplating divorce
and I must call them all, and listen to them for an hour
each, and dispense redemptive advice."

Gather your burdens in a basket in your heart. Set
them at the feet of the Mother. Say, "Take this, Great
Mama, because I cannot carry all this shit for another
minute." And then crawl into her broad lap and nestle
against her ample bosom and take a nap. When you
wake, the basket will still be there, but half its contents
will be gone, and the other half will have resumed their
ordinary shapes and sizes, no longer masquerading

as catastrophic, epic, chronic, and toxic. The Mother will clear things out and tidy up. She will take your compulsions and transmute them. But only if you freely offer them to her.

She Comes on Wings of Light

Why not?

Why not pretend for now that the Absolute (the Great Mystery, the Ground of Being) sometimes expresses itself in the body of woman? Pretending God's a dude hasn't exactly worked out for the vast majority of the human family, let alone the animal and plant communities or the air or the waters.

In the Jewish tradition (not known for its feminist history) the holiest of holy days—holier than the High Holidays themselves—is Shabbat, and she is female. Yes: the Sabbath itself is a feminine being. She is called the Shekinah, and she embodies the energies of both Malkah, the Queen, and Kallah, the Bride. She is the Holy Mother, favorite Sister, intimate Friend. She is the Beloved. In Judaism's sister tradition, Christianity, she is Sophia, Holy Wisdom.

Among a certain circle of my friends (and the family members who let me get away with it) we set aside Friday evenings to welcome the Sabbath. In the tradition of our Jewish ancestors, we imagine her as a beautiful woman who flies in through every window on wings of light, penetrating and saturating each of our hearts. Her name is Shekinah and she "resouls" us. We need the extra dose of spiritual substance she brings so that we can navigate the holy holy holy terrain of Shabbat.

Shabbat is the Hebrew word for the Sabbath. Those who come from Ashkenazi families, as I and the majority of American and European Jews do, will likely be more familiar with the Yiddish version: Shabbos. I did not learn about Shabbos from my Jewish family. I received the Sabbath transmission from the late Reb Zalman Schachter-Shalomi at

Lama Foundation, the original interspiritual community in the mountains of northern New Mexico, where Shabbat has been celebrated every single Friday since Reb Zalman first introduced it to us in the early 1980s. This is the model I still use when I celebrate Shabbat on my own, either at home or among the many communities I visit while traveling and leading interspiritual retreats. Over the years, our communal Shabbat practice at Lama has morphed into something only vaguely Jewish. But it draws on the contemplative essence of the ancient ritual and adapts it to meet both the spiritual thirst and the wariness of organized religion that characterize our times.

There are three parts to the ceremony: the blessing of the candlelight, the blessing of the wine, and the blessing of the bread.

In our community, we follow the custom in which the women—who carry the spiritual treasures and keep them safe—kindle the Sabbath lights. One candle represents *chesed* (loving-kindness) and the other *gevurah* (wise discernment). As the candles are being lighted, we cover our eyes, turning our gaze inward. "Blessed are you, Beloved our God, power of the universe, who sanctifies us with your commandments and invites us to light the candles of Shabbos." Then, integrating the indigenous wisdom of honoring earth and sky, we turn together to each of the four directions, starting with the north and ending with the west, lifting our arms and calling out to the Shekinah: "Welcome." After invoking each direction, we fold our arms at our hearts and nestle her there.

INDWELLING

The Shekinah is the indwelling feminine presence of the Divine. According to the ancient teachings, she resides in exile during the rest of the week, and on Shabbat she comes home. It is our task to receive her. It is her task to awaken us to what is real (Love) and to who we are (Love). We need to enact this ritual again and again, week after week. We are endlessly forgetting and remembering. In fact, we could look at all spiritual practices, all rituals and ceremonies and creative arts, as bells designed to wake us from the slumber of our separateness.

Nobody can seem to give me a good answer for why the Shekinah was ever sent away. It has something to do with embodiment. And the masculine religious model. As we have already seen, the world's great religions seem to have convinced themselves that the purpose of life in this world is to transcend this world, including our bodies—especially female bodies. Meanwhile, the Shekinah is about immanence, infusing all matter and all spirit with her glory. She is the shattering of the One into the blessed pandemonium of the many. She pours and spills and overflows into All That Is. She is unbounded and uncontrollable. Not good news for the prevailing power structure, whose job it is to contain and legislate. The Shekinah is subversive.

And so she is linked to missing the mark (the literal definition of the word *sin*). There's a rumor in the rabbinical literature that when Adam and Eve dared to pluck the fruit of the knowledge of good and evil, the Shekinah withdrew from creation. Another suggests that when humans forgot the truth of the one God and began misbehaving, the Holy One cast them into the desert, and she went with them. Both are narratives of separation. Which is the true meaning of sin: separation from God (or the illusion of separation from God, because that which is One cannot be divided). When we treat multiplicity as a problem and designate unity as the solution, we equate embodiment with evil. No wonder the rabbis sent the Shekinah away.

I'm not knocking Oneness. In fact, as I mentioned in the previous chapter, I have spent my life engaged in a perpetual dance of longing and union, bowing down under the weight of yearning for the Beloved and rising into the formlessness of the Divine embrace. Like my namesake, the sixteenth-century bhakti poet Mirabai, I do not perceive this love dance as a malady to be cured but rather as an opportunity to celebrate the terrible beauty of the human condition. The fire of our desire melts the boundaries that divide us from our source, and we surge back home. "For the raindrop, joy is entering the river," says the Sufi poet Ghalib.

She Turns Grapes into Wine

Which brings us to the second of the three Sabbath prayers: the *kiddush*, the blessing of the wine. The empty kiddush cup is a symbol of the heart that cries out in longing for God. The wine is the quantum response of love rushing in and filling us to overflowing. It turns out that (as all the traditions tell us) the Holy One yearns for union with us as ardently—more so!—as we desire union with the Holy One. All we need to do is lift our empty vessel, and we are instantaneously filled. On Shabbat we pour the wine to the brim so that it sloshes onto the dish beneath it and splatters the tablecloth and stains our hands. Divine Love is messy and riotous; it is intoxicating.

And love is meant to be shared. We pass the kiddush cup around. We each take a sip and wish one another "Shabbat shalom": May the peace of the angels settle on your heart; may it spread throughout the whole world. "Blessed are you, Beloved our God, who brings forth the fruit from the vine." That is, may the grapes convert into a magical potion that releases you from the tyranny of the head and brings you back to the sovereignty of the heart.

Shabbat is about reclaiming the power of love longing. Like the Bride in Solomon's Song of Songs—the startlingly sensuous book of the Torah (the Old Testament)—we rise from our bed, and, disheveled and rife with need, we rush out onto the darkened streets and plazas searching for the One who captivated and then abandoned us.

This love language is not unique to Judaism. We see it in the epic Hindu poem the Gita Govinda, where Radha, the quintessential divine lover disguised as a cowherding girl, and Krishna, the blue-skinned Lord of Love who lures the maidens with the song of his celestial flute, weave in and out of private anguish and conjugal ecstasy. We find it in the ancient Sufi story of Layla and Majnun, in which Majnun goes mad with unrequited love and takes his own life, and then, when Layla hears of his death, she dies of heartbreak. We recognize it in the bridal mysticism of Christianity, in which the soul merges with the Divine in an intimate union that dissolves the distinction of subject and object. There it is in the form of Brigid of Ireland, guardian of brides, whose triple nature blends goddesses from all over the Celtic world with a Christian saint and a folkloric figure revered for her loving touch, transforming everyday tasks into sacred realities. And we encounter it among countless indigenous communities who name twin mountain peaks after legendary lovers parted in life and reunited in the afterworld.

This dynamic tension lives inside each of us, whether or not we are in touch with it. The yearning that burns at the heart of our intimate relationships reflects the universal impulse toward union. It is at the root of our insatiable hunger to love and be loved.

The good news is that on this holy day of Shabbat, lover and Beloved are reunited. The Bride returns from exile, and the Bridegroom descends from his transcendent absorption. Heaven and earth meet and meld. The masculine and feminine aspects of the Godhead are unified, and Reality is restored to wholeness. This cosmic drama unfolds on the stage of our own souls. It shines from the candle flame and brims from the kiddush cup.

She Feeds Us with Her Body

Now it is time for the breaking of the bread. Like a shy bride, the challah, a soft, plaited bread made with eggs, oil, and a spoonful of honey, has been hiding, covered, until we have blessed the wine. Now we lift her veil and lay our hands on the braided loaf (in our house we have been known to wrap a couple of rice crackers in the decorative challah cloth or even pretzels, in a pinch). "Blessed are you, Beloved our God, who brings forth the bread from the land." We tear off pieces of the challah and feed each other from the bounty of Mother Earth.

The Earth, the Earth. Maybe we had forgotten that we belong to her. This Sabbath ritual is designed to remind us. "Our sister, Mother Earth," St. Francis calls her. On Shabbat we renew our vow to connect with and protect her, to honor and exalt her, to treat her as family.

After the Friday-evening ceremony, all of Saturday, until the sun goes down, is about hanging out with the Shekinah and laying all other distractions aside.

I have the great fortune of living in the high desert, surrounded by national forest. When I am home between frequent travels, I walk every day in the foothills behind our house. It doesn't matter if the snow is piled up to my thighs or the wind is whipping the hood off my head or the sun is frying my face: I gather my dogs, Lola and Ruby, and off we go. On Shabbat, the robust determination of my regular trek becomes a languid encounter with the body of the Mother. I slow down and remember to praise her with my footsteps. I caress her with my breath. I thank her. I may be hiking the same trails I traverse during "ordinary time," but on Shabbat I set out to walk what the Diné people (also known as Navajo) call the "Beauty Way."

In Judaism the highest *mitzvah* (which is both a blessing and a commandment) is to make love with your spouse on Shabbat. So sometime between Friday night and Saturday afternoon we are meant to reach for our beloved. This may be an earthly human, one to whom we are married, with whom we are in a committed relationship, or whose heart opens our heart enough to make us take off our clothes and merge our bodies. Or it may be with our divine Beloved who lures us with the song of an invisible flute, which on Shabbat we can follow all the way to its source, like tracing a tributary back to the mouth of the sea. On Shabbat, we have the time to rediscover our lover as the embodiment of the journey home.

At its best, Jewish wisdom affirms the body as holy and our connection to the Earth as sacred. Food, sex, art, and beauty are all evidence of the loving presence of a loving God who, on Shabbat, reveals herself as the Shekinah: indwelling, immanent, available.

She Lingers Awhile

The Sabbath is about rest, about laying down our burdens, about unhooking from the compulsions of the to-do list. On Shabbat, said the twentieth-century spiritual activist Rabbi Abraham Joshua Heschel, we build a temple in time and take refuge there. "Six days a week we live under the tyranny of things of space; on the Sabbath we try to become attuned to holiness in time. It is a day on which we are called upon to share in what is eternal . . . to turn from the results of creation to the mystery of creation; from the world of creation to the creation of the world."

Eve Ilsen, Reb Zalman's widow, spoke to me about the femininity inherent in this time of "not doing." We have prepared with care, making food ahead of time so that our labors are light when the Sabbath comes. It is a deeply receptive time, quintessentially feminine, sensual, fecund. Shabbat is the time of the spiritual zygote, Eve says, a fusion of the DNA of the feminine and masculine principles of the universe, form and formlessness, earth and heaven. "An egg without receiving sperm is just an egg."

For me, Shabbat is both a contemplative practice and an act of social and environmental justice. It is contemplative in that taking a Sabbath from our quotidian lives is synonymous with showing up for whatever arises, moment by moment, with heightened attention and availability. On Shabbos, I unplug from electronic devices and break my addiction to communications. The messages pile up, but the sky does not fall. When I testify to the bountiful fruits of this custom, many of my friends and students explain to me that they are way too busy (substitute *important*) to take off an entire day a week. They cannot afford it. There are too many demands battering at the doors of their life. Too many emails and texts and Instagram posts to respond to—and to respond to immediately! Spaciousness feels like laziness, looks like boredom, smells like danger.

I used to feel the same way. I would light the candles on Friday and say, "Hi" to the Shekinah, but by Saturday morning I was back to my old trick of trying to run the world. Keeping the Sabbath holy has taught me that I cannot afford *not* to observe Shabbat. And the Universe graciously expands the container of time to hold my practice and support my rest.

Keeping the Sabbath holy can also be a revolutionary act. Engaged as a practice of voluntary simplicity, it can subvert capitalism. From sunset on Friday to sunset on Saturday I try not to spend money, burn fossil fuels, or otherwise contribute to the pattern of overconsumption to which privileged Western white people like me have grown inured. I am endeavoring to lighten my carbon footprint. I approach this day as a Sabbath from feeding the machine of commerce that is responsible for bulldozing the lives of those on the margins and causing terrible suffering. The Shekinah opens my ears so that I can hear the cries of the world.

She Returns to Exile

How could she leave us? Shabbat is a taste of *Olam haBa*, "the world to come" in Hebrew. She is so sweet and delicious, so blessed and sublime, that we cannot bear to be parted from her when the sun sets on Saturday. And so the Holy One, it is said, in her infinite mercy, grants us not the standard twenty-four hours but twenty-five. We are given an extra hour to get used to the fact that we must return to the world of working and consuming, producing and manipulating. It's not that these things are inherently bad; it's that they tend to lead us away from her and so from our felt interconnection with All That Is.

There is a ritual for this, too. It's called *Havdalah*. At the closing of Shabbat we gather again and light a special braided candle, symbolizing that sacred and ordinary time are intertwined. The two flames merge. Then we bless the wine. Next—and the soul poetry of this part slays me—we inhale from a box of fragrant spices so that we will not faint with sorrow that Shabbat is over and the Shekinah is returning to exile. Finally, we share the sanctified wine and save a few drops to douse the flame with. We wistfully bid her farewell.

Shabbat is about harmony. It's about restoring balance—the balance between the masculine and feminine aspects of our own souls and the balance of power between women and men. It's about building community and remembering our interdependence with each other and with the Earth herself, taking responsibility for our habits of consumption and allowing ourselves to rest and recharge. Shabbat is about forging a direct relationship with the Shekinah, the feminine face of God. It's about taking refuge in her arms.

Her time of exile is over now. We do not need to keep sending her away. We are called now to reinstate the feminine to her rightful place in our lives, in our relationships, and throughout creation. She belongs here and it's time to celebrate her presence, draw on her strength, drink in her consolation, and let her guide us in repairing the world.

deepening

Set aside a regular day—once a week, a day a month, a weekend—as a Sabbath. It is, of course, not necessary to follow the Jewish tradition of Shabbat, which begins with lighting the candles on Friday evening and ends with Havdalah at sunset on Saturday. Pick your own time frame and find your own way to keep the Sabbath holy. The important thing is to cultivate a regular practice of laying aside all daily concerns and letting yourself rest.

Read, write poetry, color in a coloring book, take a hike, make a beautiful meal and feed your loved ones—anything that reconnects you with your soul. Keep a journal of your experiences so that you can reflect back to yourself the gifts that arise when you open the door to deep rest and loving attention to the moment. (If you choose to write, see "Writing Practice Guidelines" on page 223.)

The heart breaks open
A dried branch bursts into bloom
Light comes pouring in

 3

BREAKING OPEN

The Alchemy of Longing

opening

So far, this incarnation has been fraught with losses, rife with disappointments, heavy with heartache. There have been untimely deaths of loved ones who seemed to be about to cross the threshold into a beautiful and interesting life, not out of it. Serious health diagnoses that changed the way you navigate space, relate to food, see your self-image. Love affairs that once contained all the seeds of your joy and then withered before your eyes. Hands on your body that had no right to be there, making you mistrust the hands you really wanted on your body. Betrayals by colleagues or cousins, financial ruin, debilitating addictions.

When you breathe into the pain of your losses, you detect the presence of a smoldering ember you thought had been snuffed out years ago. But there it is, fragrant and warm. If you blew on it now it would burst into flame. Longing. Longing for God. You don't even believe in God anymore. Not as a personified entity that grants wishes and smacks you down. And yet this burning yearning has never really gone away. In your broken-open state you remember what it feels like to feel separate from the One, to want union, to want it with every fiber of your being. This longing confounds you, and you don't know what to do with it so you press it back down.

At first, you will not recognize the radiance hidden in all the darkness that has befallen you. The grief, the longing. You will not be equipped with the skills required to translate the secret Welcome Home sign planted in your soul's ravaged landscape; it will look like Keep Out. If someone were to tell you that your losses were your passage to a voyage across the sea of samsara, the suffering of illusion, to the land of Nirvana, the bliss of awakening, you would not believe them. Even if twenty people—or a hundred—told you this pain was a blessing, you would not believe them (you might want to hurt them). You will think you are doing it wrong, that your suffering is not redemptive; it is messy and awkward. Unspiritual.

Your discovery of the restorative root system underlying your ruined life will come later, in the inevitable springtime, when the small green shoots of compassion muscle their way up and out of the charred earth and begin to spread and bud and flower and propagate themselves. You will eat, because you will be hungry. And then you will feed the world, because you will not be able to resist the impulse to share the bounty.

The Cry of Separation

> Listen to the reed and the tale it tells,
> how it sings of separation:
> Ever since they cut me from the reed bed,
> my wail has caused men and women to weep.
> I want a heart that is torn open with longing
> so that I might share the pain of this love.
> Whoever has been parted from his source
> longs to return to that state of union.   RUMI

Sometimes it appears as if it is only when we are most radically shattered that the boundless grace of divine Love comes pouring in. Loss is a fire that takes down everything extraneous, including our cherished beliefs. We must be stripped of all our opinions on the matter if we hope to have a naked encounter with the truth of divine Love. Our annihilation is both the necessary and the sufficient condition for the privilege of union with the source of divine Love.

I did not come up with this system.

I might have designed things differently.

And yet I suggest that we shift our perspective from the familiar and macho lens of retribution to the more feminine frame of compassion. Our loved ones did not die because we required a wake-up call. Our marriages do not go up in flames as a result of our pesky little attachments. We do not endure sexual abuse and institutional oppression on account of our dualistic preconceptions.

Shit happens.

This is the human condition. Incarnation involves being separated from what we love sometimes and other times having to put up with things we'd do anything to get away from. The Buddha told us this. But he also told us that we could search the whole world and we would never find anyone—not a single being—who is not also engaged in this dance of clinging and aversion. It is by showing up for the full encounter with reality that we discover our hidden wholeness, which was, of course, present all along.

MUSTARD SEED

Which reminds me of a story. It's about how we can take refuge in the human experience, how there's power in that truth. You may know this one. But like any good tale, it stays alive and seems relevant each time we tell it. Here's my version.

During the lifetime of the Buddha, there was a young mother named Kisa Gotami, who went crazy with grief when her child died. Kisa careened through the streets of her village, begging everyone in her path to give her the medicine that would bring her child back to life.

But there is no cure for death.

Her neighbors were sympathetic, though they had no access to such a magical potion. If they had, their own loved ones would still be alive. Yet their dead remained dead.

Finally someone encouraged Kisa to make a pilgrimage to the Buddha and ask him to restore her son's life. And so she did. Carrying the body of her child in her arms, Kisa made her way to the forest where the Awakened One was teaching the dharma. When the distraught young woman broke into the clearing and dropped to her knees at the feet of the master, he suspended his discourse and gave her his full attention.

"Please, Great One, they told me you could bring my baby back to life."

The Buddha's eyes filled with tears (as they were wont to do whenever he beheld the pain of the world), and then he closed them for a long moment. "Try this," he said, opening his eyes again. "Return to your village. Gather a mustard seed from every household that has not been touched by death. With these seeds I will concoct a remedy that will bring your son back to life."

Mute with anticipation, Kisa shifted the burden of her child's body from one shoulder to the other and raced back to her village. She knocked on every door. But everywhere she went, whoever greeted her at the door was compelled to admit that, while they would have gladly contributed to her cause, they did not meet the Buddha's only criterion, for someone they had loved had also died.

When Kisa had knocked on the last door at the outskirts of the village and learned that the inhabitants of that house, too, had been touched by death, her fractured heart cracked all the way open. She lay her baby's corpse on the ground beside her, and she prostrated herself in the dirt. She wept, and she screamed. She tore her sari and clawed her own breasts. Exhausted, she grew still. And then she got it. What breaks our hearts is also what connects us: the exquisite impermanence of the phenomenal world; our longing to keep what we love the same forever; and our desire for that which we can't stand to go away and never come back. It is the same way for everyone. And Kisa got that it wouldn't hurt if we didn't love and that love is worth the pain. That even knowing that loss is inevitable she would not hesitate to love all over again, love with her eyes wide open, her heart wide open, her mind as present and spacious as the horizon.

Acceptance, Kisa realized, does not mean *not caring* that terrible things happen. Of course we care! We must care. Caring is what rescues us from the lie that this world is nothing but an illusion to be transcended. Caring links us to the world as a crucible for cooking up the elixir of mercy. Acceptance means being with things as they are, not turning away and not trying to shape them to our will. This renders it possible to make of our pain an offering of love. This blesses all ground as sacred ground.

Kisa Gotami buried her baby and returned to the Buddha's grove. She became one of his most cherished and awakened disciples. Unlike most of his colleagues, the Buddha accepted women students. Not only did he believe that women are as capable as men of attaining liberation, but maybe he also saw us as uniquely shaped to navigate the Great Way, because our two wings of loving-kindness and wise discernment are especially balanced. We can lift off and soar. And we can make a safe landing. We know how to enter the heart of every kind of suffering and stay with it until it gives way to any kind of awakening.

Reclaim Longing

I have always been struck by how much loss resembles longing. Grief strips us of attachment to things that do not really matter (how my butt looks in a pair of jeans, for instance, or whether my work is acknowledged in the way I'd hoped). Grief reorders our priorities, reconfigures our values. Grief dispenses with bullshit and replaces it with emptiness. Please do not confuse emptiness here with lack. The classic Buddhist concept of *sunyata* is actually closer in meaning to "boundlessness." At least that's how my friend Joan Halifax, a Zen *roshi* (priest), translates it.

It is this sacred spaciousness that most spiritual technologies, engineered over millennia and across the religious spectrum, have been designed to uncover. Nakedness of soul. With the garments of our habitual attachments in a pile on the ground at our feet and our sense of self in tatters, we can step into the arms of the Beloved.

Which is usually the last thing on our minds at times like these. When we are grieving, we are not interested in ecstatic union. We long for our dead baby to come back to life. We ache for our ex-spouse to stop loving that new person and resume loving us. We desperately want the blood test to be revealed as a false positive so we can get on with our life as it was, climbing mountains and saving the world. In fact, it would be monstrous to suggest that someone in the throes of fresh loss seize it as an opportunity to consummate her longing and make love with the Divine.

It is only gradually and tenderly that we may begin to breathe into the shattered space of grief and catch the fragrance of the holy that is wafting on the breeze of our abandonment. Little by little, when we are weary enough to stop trying to fix our brokenness, we may glimpse the unbrokenness that undergirds the catastrophe of our loss. We recognize that the charged atmosphere of a loved one's dying feels just like the charged atmosphere when a baby is born. The pain of missing loved ones who have died, or a way of life that has ended, occupies a similar region of the heart where spiritual longing resides.

These boundary lands of life and death are bathed in beauty. This is where we are closest to our source, which is Love. It's as if the heat of our grieving becomes a catalyst for mending our soul's broken connection to the Divine. Grief can open the door to holy desire, which in turn leads us into the arms of that which we yearn for.

Mystics seem to have no shame about contradicting themselves left and right. They blithely proclaim that the cure for pain is in the pain itself and that the cry of longing is the sigh of merging. That's because the path of the mystic reconciles contradictory propositions (such as harrowing sorrow and radical amazement) and blesses us with an expanded capacity to sit with ambiguity, to treasure vulnerability, to celebrate paradox as the highest truth. If we lean toward the anguish of grief and soften into the ache of missing the ones we love or of regretting the unfinished business between us, we may recognize the presence of the sacred permeating the field of the heart. Rather than pushing away uncomfortable feelings of yearning for that which we have lost—or maybe never had but pine for nonetheless—what about letting our hearts break all the way open?

Modern Western culture conditions us to step away from that precipice as quickly as possible. We are conditioned to see death and painful longing as problems to be solved rather than as sacred landscapes to be revered. We are encouraged to medicate our grief, to treat loss as a malfunction that needs troubleshooting, to satisfy our longing as swiftly as possible. We may feel obliged to employ any of dozens of spiritual methods, from meditating ourselves into a trance to conjuring up "the power of positive thinking," in order to bypass our direct experiences. We buy into some bullshit notion of "the law of attraction," which asserts that difficult life experiences are the result of faulty beliefs and that if we simply focus on what we want, the Universe will fall into place to meet our every need and grant our every wish. From this perspective, we can't help but consider loss and longing as cruel and unruly, judging ourselves to be doing something wrong when we fail to get away from the pain.

Believe me, I am not a fan of tragic loss. I hate that my beautiful, blossoming fourteen-year-old daughter, Jenny, crashed my car and died (I talk more about her in chapter 11). It hasn't been easy to witness loved ones suffering mightily as cancer ravaged their bodies, trapping them in its clutches and not letting them go until there was nothing left of them. I am a peace activist; I vigorously oppose the culture of death that manifests in the form of war. I embrace all that is life-affirming: poetry, art, healthy food, connection with nature, community.

But with this kind of messaging that pathologizes death and loss, of course many of us are going to mistake the fire of grief or longing for what we cannot have or can no longer have—for problems to be resolved—rather than as evidence of our holy membership in the human condition and an invitation to spiritual transformation. By "transformation" I do not mean transcendence (as you may have guessed by now). I mean the *opposite* of rising above the realities of this world. Rather, it's about becoming so fully present that the line between sacred and ordinary is obliterated and the face of the Beloved shines from every face—humans, bees, juniper trees.

The Terrible Grace of Love Longing

The Dagger

The Dark One threw me a glance like a dagger today.
Since that moment, I am insane; I can't find my body.
The pain has gone through my arms and legs,
    and I can't find my mind.
At least three of my friends are completely mad.
I know the thrower of daggers well; he enjoys
    roving the woods.
The partridge loves the moon; and the lamplight
    pulls in the moth.
You know, for the fish, water is precious; without it,
    the fish dies.
If he is gone, how shall I live? I can't live without him.
Go and speak to the dagger-thrower:
    Say, Mira belongs to you.   MIRABAI

The poet-mystics of all traditions celebrate the transformational power of grief and loss and the terrible grace of love longing. My namesake, Mirabai, is an example of the alchemy of heartbreak. Mirabai lived during the same spiritually fertile time as the Spanish mystics I love, John of the Cross and Teresa of Ávila, but in a very different place. Mirabai was a devotional, or *bhakti*, poet from North India who relinquished wealth and status to track the invisible footprints of Krishna, the elusive Lord of Love. She wasn't trying to be subversive. She didn't stage a political action. She simply followed the music of love longing resounding in her heart. Sometimes it sounded like the roar of separation; other times, like a song of homecoming, a lullaby of belonging.

This inner music led Mira from the comfort of the family palace to the local village streets and riverbanks, where she sang and danced with anyone who would sing and dance with her without a whit of regard for socioeconomic status or religious affiliation. She welcomed high-caste scholars and untouchables with equal warmth. Hindus, Jains, and Muslims, traditionally separated by entrenched ideologies, were universally drawn to the beauty of Mira's rapturous poetry and *bhajans* (devotional songs). Everyone resonated with the purity of her passion.

Mira's relationship with her Beloved was not all drenched in bliss. Quite the opposite. Most of the time Mira was on fire with desire for Krishna, the one who had toyed with her heart from the day she first met him. From time to time he would reveal himself and then slip back into the shadows, enfold her in a mystical embrace and then sneak away while she was sleeping. Sometimes she felt close to him, but most of the time he eluded her grasp. I call this the Disappearing God Syndrome. It plagues and blesses mystics of every kind, but it is the poets who best express the paradoxical pain and joy of longing.

"ONE TO ME IS FAME AND SHAME"

Mira refused to let her public's adoration go to her head or familial scorn bring her to her knees. "One to me is fame and shame," she declared in more than one poem. This did not stop her husband's family from condemning her—nor thousands of spiritual seekers from following her. Mira's admirers may have included the legendary poet-mystic Kabir, beloved by Hindus, Muslims, and Sikhs, and likely also included the third Mughal emperor, Akbar. It was Akbar who stirred up a hornet's nest of trouble at the royal house where the young Mira lived with her husband and his family. Knowing of the hatred Mira's Hindu in-laws harbored for Muslims, the emperor disguised himself as a beggar and made a pilgrimage to pay homage to the young poet-saint of whom all of North India was speaking. Deeply moved by her singing, Akbar left a priceless jeweled necklace at her feet. When the family discovered this treasure and realized who had been sitting in their midst, they banished Mira from the household.

This was not her first conflict with her husband's people nor her last banishment. Their association started off with a fundamental difference in opinion about the meaning of marriage. Mira had been betrothed to Prince Bhoj Raj for most of her life, as was—and in some places still is—the custom in India, and she was obliged to marry him when she was a teenager. The problem was, in her heart Mira was already married to Krishna. When she was a child, a family friend had gifted her with a small statue of the blue-skinned love god, and she was smitten. She carried her little lover with her everywhere, fed him milk from her own cup, and nestled him beside her on the pillow all night. Her heart had been Krishna's from that moment onward, and so when the time came to consummate her arranged marriage, she found it impossible to give herself to her earthly husband.

Prince Bhoj Raj was not pleased about this, and his family was furious. He cajoled her; they threatened her. Mirabai went through the motions of a high-caste Hindu wife, but she burst into poetry and song at the slightest whiff of her Beloved, whose fragrance permeated her being. Mira writes about the various ways they tried to get rid of her. Her mother-in-law offered Mira nectar laced with poison. She drank it and found the concoction sweet and refreshing. Her father-in-law sent her a garland of flowers with a venomous snake hidden inside the blossoms. The serpent turned into a spray of lilacs.

After three years of domestic charade, Mirabai's husband went off to fight the Mughals and was killed in battle. It was Mira's duty to commit *suttee*, to burn herself alive on her husband's funeral pyre. But since she considered Krishna to be her spouse and not Prince Bhoj Raj, she saw no reason to participate in such a violent act. She refused and was again exiled, this time for good. That suited her perfectly. Mira spent the rest of her life as a wandering minstrel, singing and dancing for her Beloved, and wherever she went people joined the stream of her ecstatic devotion and let themselves be carried into the arms of the One.

Which is all very nice. But the underlying story of Mirabai is a story of spiritual warriorship. This is a woman who defied social norms so powerful that her defiance could have cost her her life. Not only did she voluntarily renounce her inherited privilege to worship among the poor, but she lived as an exemplar of an empowered woman who chose the path of Love over convention, of poetry over luxury, of homelessness over imprisonment in the expectations of society. Mirabai offered herself to the alchemical flames of longing for God and was transfigured. Her example of abdicating social advantages for the sake of spiritual transformation is as relevant today as it ever was.

That's why those of us who have shoes must take them off now and recognize that we are standing on holy ground. That's why we who can afford to speak out need to risk unmasking the fake little gods worshipped by a culture of war and praise the God of Love with all our hearts, and with our minds and with our bodies. The brave women mystics who walked before us show us the way.

The Long Drought Is Over

My Beloved has come home with the rains,
And the fire of longing is doused.
Now is the time for singing, the time of union.
At the first thunderclap,
Even the peacocks open their tails with pleasure
     and dance.
Giridhara is in my courtyard, and my wandering
     heart has returned.
Like lilies that blossom under the full moon's light,
I open to him in this rain: every pore of my body
     is cooled.
Mira's separation and torment are over.
He who comes to those who love has remembered
     his promise. MIRABAI

Love Language

Mirabai wasn't the only one borrowing the language of love to express the pain of separation. We saw, a few pages back in this chapter, how the poetry of Rumi (a feminine mystic in the body of a man) knocks on the door of the heart to invite us into a special relationship with suffering as a portal to grace. This is the entire plot line of the Song of Songs, too, that peculiarly erotic biblical scripture in which the Bride—archetype for the soul in love with the Divine—writhes in the throes of longing for her runaway Bridegroom. Ultimately, he arrives at the door of her mother's house, and the mother slips away so that the lovers may consummate in peace. In passion, actually. By the time the Bridegroom shows up, they are both so drenched in yearning that the doorknob drips with "sweet flowing myrrh." As with many of Mirabai's poems, in the Song of Songs the story crosses the threshold of longing into the ecstasy of union.

> At night on my bed I longed for my only love.
> I sought him, but did not find him.
> I must rise and go about the city,
> the narrow streets and squares, till I find my only love.
> I sought him everywhere but I could not find him.
> SONG OF SONGS 3:1–2

> Bind me as a seal upon your heart,
> A sign upon your arm,
> For love is as fierce as death . . .
> Even its sparks are a raging fire,
> A devouring flame.
> SONG OF SONGS 8:6

The Hindu epic poem the Gita Govinda, composed by Jayadeva in the twelfth century, is another spectacularly sensual piece in which any distinction between spiritual longing and sexual desire becomes irrelevant. The Gita Govinda describes the love antics of Lord Krishna, who gives himself to Radha, his divine consort in the form of a milkmaid (*gopi*). Then he messes around with all the other milkmaids—every single one of them, making love to each in whatever way she most particularly desires. But when Radha rebuffs him, he pines for her. In the end they make their way home to each other's hearts, to each other's bodies, and meld in ecstatic union, which is all the sweeter for their having suffered separation.

The lush language invokes the ache of the soul's need to return to her source: Love. Here we have a taste of Radha's urgency:

> [She] declares each step she takes is to your feet: what fire the moon is when you've turned away: In Mādhava she dreads the love-god's arrows: apart and miserable, she thinks of you.

And here is a glimpse of Krishna's desperation:

> Around and round about he sighs and watches, and fights, as bees in thickets, for his breath, and makes, remakes the bed, and still he watches: tired, by love bewildered, still he waits.

And this is what their fulfillment looks like:

> Pressed round by arms, by breasts, by fingernails, by pounding hips, by teeth on lips, his head pulled down but mad to have the honeyed stream: how curiously will lovers take their joy.

In both the Western and the Eastern versions of this great love story, the lovers start off together, and then they are riven apart, and then they find their way back to each other. The journey of return can be harrowing. In fact, grief is the philosopher's stone that transmutes the lead of longing into the gold of union. Wholeness is the healing herb that grows from the soil of loss. Myth upon myth, in culture after culture, from age to age, speaks to the power of romantic love to convey the relationship between the individual being and the One.

Something in our souls recognizes this dynamic of exile and return. We remember that our source is Love. We suffer from the illusion of having been pulled up from our soul roots. We long to go home. We engage every practice we can get our hands on to restore our birthright of belonging. And when we attain those fleeting moments of union, we realize we were never two to begin with. We were always one and always will be one.

The language of love is like a spaceship that blasts us through the layers of illusion and delivers us to the truth of our essential connectedness with the Divine and our interconnectedness with all of creation. There's nothing like a passage of mystical poetry, incandescent with the fire of longing and besotted by the wine of union, to evoke our own burning yearning and reveal our capacity for melding.

This is why I have spent my life in the company of the mystics of every spiritual tradition. This is why I tuck a volume of the sky-clad poet Lalla or Shakespeare's sonnets into my backpack when I hike, along with the apples and chocolate and sunscreen. Life in a separate body is a constant opportunity to forget who I am (the chosen lover of the Holy One, just like you). A good poem wakes me up, kissing my eyelids, when I drift back to sleep.

It's not as if falling in love with the Divine rescues us from the travails of the human condition. Our partners betray us sometimes, and our dead remain dead. It's that keeping the heart open, even in hell, makes space for the Beloved. It is in the darkest nights of our souls, when all we know is that we know nothing, that the presence of the sacred may quietly well up, mingling with our pain and connecting us to a love that will never die.

deepening

In her spiritual autobiography, *The Book of My Life*,
Teresa of Ávila engages in a bold and intimate prayer:

> "Why isn't it enough for you, my Lord," I
> complained, "to keep me bound to this
> miserable life? For love of you, I endure all this
> and resign myself to living in a place where
> everything hinders me from enjoying you. Here
> I have to eat and sleep and conduct business
> and carry on conversations with everyone. It
> torments me, my Lord, but I suffer it all for
> love of you. In the few moments I have left
> over to enjoy your presence, how could you
> hide from me, my Beloved? Is this compatible
> with your compassion? How can your love for
> me allow this? . . . Do not put up with this
> separation a moment longer, my Beloved! I beg
> you to see how much you are hurting the one
> who loves you so much!"

What do you want from the Holy One? Write a
letter to your Beloved, stating your demands. Don't
censor yourself. When you are finished, read it to
someone you trust. Make them promise not to offer
any feedback, negative or positive, but simply to listen,
bearing witness.

Now the horizon is clear
Fire has swept it all away
One small bird comes home

▷◁▷◁▷◁

MELTING DOWN

Dissolving into the One

opening

Ever since you first tasted the elixir of nobodyness,
maybe in the midst of meditating or grieving, you
have lost your hunger for somebodyness. Mainstream
culture conditioned you to construct a persona
and defend it with all your might. The endless self-
improvement project, fueled by self-loathing and
foiled by the realities of the human condition, has only
reinforced the illusion that you are separate from your
Source. But a combination of spiritual practice and
tragic losses ended that game. You, for one, are relieved
to surrender.

Your surrender is invisible. You still go through the
motions of promoting your work on social media; you
make an effort to limit your carbs, practice yoga, pick
out interesting things to wear. But that's not because
you actually identify as an individual being, detached
from all other beings or from the Earth or from
the Holy One. You have come to understand that a
functioning ego is a necessary vessel for an incarnate
soul. You don't regard your ego as a problem. You just

don't take it seriously. (Which used to piss your ego off, given its self-important nature. But she's getting used to it.)

When you were young you recognized Ultimate Reality as Beloved, and you developed a powerful crush. Over the decades your roles reversed and reversed again. You were the seeker; you were the sought. Eventually, in moments of deep stillness or unbearable anguish, lover and Beloved melded. Only Love remained. This state of suchness looked like emptiness but felt like plenitude. You came to understand that not only have you been connected to your Beloved all along but you are that which you had been seeking.

You had expected God to be the prize you would collect after all the hard work of seeking God. It turns out that the object you thought of as *you* does not exist, which means the subject you called God is not real either.

You would have anticipated such an insight to be devastating, but it isn't. It's amusing. Chuckling at the cosmic joke, you get on with business. There are temples to build, curricula to develop, sonatas to compose, start-ups to start up. You did not buy your equanimity cheaply. Frequent firestorms eradicated your opinion on the matter. Multiple meltdowns led you to a place where your only option was to melt. Who knew that dissolving would be so sweet?

Shakti

The dismantling of our false structures is holy work, and it's inextricable from creativity. The phoenix is born from the ashes. Resurrection does not happen without crucifixion. In Hindu mythology, Shakti is the primal energy of the Universe. She is the embodiment of power and strength coursing through creation, animating and enlivening all that is. All forms are manifestations of Shakti. She is the Great Mother. She is the source from which all the other goddesses spring. She is also the fiery solvent that sometimes, either spontaneously or in response to certain spiritual practices, flows into the soul and dissolves the boundaries of the separate self, restoring our essential unity with the Supreme Being.

Shakti is the consort of Shiva, god of destruction and transformation. This relationship does not in any way imply her subservience. There could be no Shiva without Shakti; they are intertwined and interdependent. While Shiva represents the transcendent nature of the divine reality, Shakti is immanence. She is the force of embodiment, the Word made flesh, the big bang. Shakti is not only the movement of the One into the many, she is also liberation from the illusion of separation.

KUNDALINI

One of Shakti's favorite forms is kundalini. She resides in the subtle body, coiled as a serpent at the base of the spine, the root chakra. Spiritual practices like meditation and visualization, breathing exercises and chanting can rouse this slumbering life-force. Then, like a bolt of electricity, Shakti rises, radiant, unwinding through each chakra, waking and lighting it up, bursting at last through the thousand-petaled lotus of the crown chakra. In this way, Shakti merges with Shiva, pure consciousness. The manifest melts into the unmanifest and then descends back into form, in an ever-unfolding cosmic dance of becoming and dissolving.

This is not as rarefied a state as it may sound. Like any mystical experience, the awakening of the kundalini is our birthright. There are countless moments in our lives when, in states of profound prayer or art making, of sorrow or lovemaking, we naturally step out of our own way and become a clear channel for the primordial power of creation to flow.

This power is the feminine. She is creative, she is wild, and she does not require permission to blast through our being and use us. In tantric philosophy, which emphasizes our relationship with Shakti and recognizes the potency of kundalini, rather than endeavoring to transcend embodied experience, we are guided to harness the energy of life to fuel our awakening.

Some kundalini experiences are dramatic and bequeath to us increased access to ecstatic states for the rest of our lives. Others feel more ordinary. They change us in some ongoing way, yes, but they are more integrated with the tapestry of our days, rather than standing alone as peak experiences.

My friend Dorothy Walters is an example of a spontaneous and utterly transformative kundalini awakening. Dorothy was a college professor of English and women's studies in Kansas when, at the age of fifty-three and with no context for what was happening, her kundalini suddenly ascended, uprooting life as she knew it and catapulting her onto a path of longing and ecstasy. This formerly political, academic woman became a raving mystic. Now, at ninety, Dorothy still pays attention to the suffering of the world and seeks to alleviate it, but she mostly spends her days writing poetry worthy of the great mystic poets of the past, such as Rumi and Mirabai. To read Dorothy's poems to the Beloved is not only to bear witness to her experience of divine union but to participate in the direct experience of Love.

Devotion

There are human beings, like the great Indian saint Neem Karoli Baba (whom devotees lovingly call Maharaj-ji), who seem to be especially clear channels for Shakti and whose very presence helps awaken the consciousness and open the hearts of everyone around them. I never had a chance to meet Maharaj-ji in the flesh. But I don't even remember a time when he was not my window into God. I was nine years old when Ram Dass's iconic book *Be Here Now* came out and connected this remarkable holy man from the Himalayas to millions of Western seekers, among them my parents and my friends' parents, my teachers and neighbors in our countercultural community. This must be what Jesus is like for other people: the sacred ground they grew from and walk upon, the touchstone, home base.

Shortly before his sudden death on September 11, 1973 (when I was twelve), Maharaj-ji abruptly stopped his lifelong practice of writing "RAM RAM RAM" in his little diary and handed it to one of his closest disciples, Siddhi Ma (later called Mata-ji, "beloved mother"), instructing her to continue the repetition of the divine name. After he was gone, it became clear this was his signal that Siddhi Ma was to carry his lineage, to care for his disciples, his temples, and his devotional teachings.

For many years, the "Ma's" (the Indian women devoted to Maharaj-ji) had kept to themselves in the backrooms of his ashrams, and the Westerners hardly knew they existed. But there they were, tending Maharaj-ji's every physical need behind the scenes so that he could tend his followers' every spiritual need out front. With humility and good humor, Mata-ji gathered Maharaj-ji's far-flung family into her arms after he was gone, and she kept us there until her own death at the end of 2017.

In October 2010, on the ninth anniversary of my daughter's passing, I made a pilgrimage to the Kainchi Ashram, the main temple where Maharaj-ji had given *darshan* (the beholding of the Divine in the form of the guru) to westerners in the early 1970s and where Mata-ji still resided in the warm months. The ashram is nestled in the foothills of the Himalayas in the northernmost part of India. It is less than one hundred miles from New Delhi, yet it takes more than ten hours by car to wind up through the dramatic mountain passes and down into the Kumaon Valley.

Being in Kainchi feels like stepping back in time a thousand years. And being with Mata-ji felt like a homecoming.

After the loss of my daughter, my road had been harrowing. Although nearly a decade had unfolded, I arrived with a tattered soul and a shattered heart. It wasn't that Sri Siddhi Ma had some kind of magical powers to mend me (perhaps), or that she possessed a metaphysical vision to see beyond this world (could be), or even that she lavished me with sympathy (she didn't). It was simple: she looked at me with full attention, and she saw me truly. That's what happens when a person shows up for you with their full presence. They see you. And to be fully seen is a rare and transformative gift. It seems to me that the capacity for true presence we find among awakened beings is an artifact of their own annihilation: their identification with a separate self has dissolved in the ocean of the One. All that is left is pure presence.

Sitting with Mata-ji and singing to her, prostrating myself at her feet and watching her *pranam* (bow) before the temple goddesses, melted my cynicism about gurus and allowed my inclination toward reverence to flower. Yet what was most true and real for me about this magnificent woman was not the devotion she elicited in me but, rather, her devotion to Maharaj-ji. Sri Siddhi Ma embodied the guru-disciple relationship and lit it up for all to see and feel and taste. Everything for Mata-ji pointed back to Maharaj-ji. Every good thing belonged to him, and every suffering was an opportunity to follow the trail of fire directly into the garden of his love.

DIE BEFORE YOU DIE

The mystics of all traditions and both sexes sing of the joy of burning. What burns? Our attachment to the false self. The illusion of separation from the Divine. "Die before you die," said the prophet Muhammad (and also the masterful teacher of the nondual, Ramana Maharshi). Rumi spoke of the blessing of being a trampled grape and becoming the wine of the Beloved or of being a chickpea the Great Chef keeps knocking back into the pot whenever it leaps for the rim. The bhakti poet Mirabai extolled the crazy wisdom of the partridge "who swallows hot coals for love of the moon."

Our mistake as postmodern citizens of the Western world is to equate self-emptying (known as kenosis in the Christian mystical tradition) with a self-esteem problem. When the mystics aspire to become nothing, we cringe. After all, we have worked hard in therapy to recover from emotional abuse and reconstruct a robust sense of our own worth. Seminars on "prosperity consciousness" and the so-called "law of attraction" are a booming business. We write little affirmations for ourselves and tape them to our bathroom mirrors or slip them into a specially designated "God Box." We are encouraged to have *boundaries*; we encourage others to have *boundaries*.

Boundaries can shut out the Holy One and trap us inside an illusory experience of separation. What about this? Let the margins melt. The way of the mystic is the way of surrender, of dying to the false self to be reborn as the true Self, the God Self, the radiant, divine being we actually are. It's not that the old self—the personality, the ego, the stories we tell about our lives—is bad or wrong. It's that when we recognize the essential emptiness of our individual identity in light of the glorious gift of our interconnectedness with the One, independence becomes much less compelling. <u>And that's the path of the feminine: the path of connection.</u>

THE WAY OF THE LITTLE FLOWER

Connecting sometimes requires dying. The feminine mystic is okay with that.

The more awake and available we can be to all parts of our lives, the more gracefully and graciously we can die. We sacrifice ourselves on a thousand altars, large and small, when we dare wrest our Beloved out of the clutches of rigid belief systems and reclaim our intimacy with the One or when we raise our feminine voice and stand up for Mother Earth. We die each time our children encounter cruelty or illness. Every betrayal is a death, every shattered illusion, every breakup of a relationship. Most mystical traditions will remind us that the way we navigate these endings informs the way we leave this world.

The annihilation of the false self does not have to be harsh, violent, painful. That is the masculine way: to wage war on our delusions. Rather than struggling to override the individual ego, the feminine mystic celebrates interconnection. It can be a simple matter of recognizing our smallness in the face of the awesome majesty of creation. This shift in perspective does not mean that we don't count or that our actions do not matter. It means we can relax and do our best to contribute something beautiful to the vast cosmos we share.

"It isn't necessary to do great things but rather to do small things with great love," said the twentieth-century humanitarian Mother Teresa of Calcutta, paraphrasing the nineteenth-century French mystic Thérèse of Lisieux. Thérèse's dedication to offering the essence of everyday experience to the glory of God characterized the entirety of her brief incarnation. She referred to herself as "a little flower" in the garden of the Divine, no more important or less magnificent than any other. To be a simple daisy in the divine flower bed is a magnificent thing! A blessed thing.

Although Thérèse was a champion of spiritual nakedness, this did not mean she was passive. Thérèse cultivated her awakening with every fiber of her courageous heart. From the time she could remember, all she ever wanted was to be a saint. Her childhood wish came true. Thérèse died of tuberculosis at age twenty-four, resplendent with physical suffering, ravaged by holy doubt, crazy in love with God. An abundance of miracles following her death, involving spontaneous healings experienced by those who prayed to her and accompanied by the fragrance of roses, is attributed to this saint of holy humility.

Thérèse's greatness lies in her smallness. The "little flower" continues to strew the path with beauty, reminding us to disappear into the Great Garden, where we find our true being. Each time we resist the temptation to buy some shiny new thing or defend ourselves against false accusations, whenever we choose simplicity over complexity or being kind over being right, we peel off another layer separating us from Love itself.

Kali

> As the radiant blackness of divine mystery,
> she plays through the lotus wilderness of the
>   sacred human body.
> The practitioner of meditation encounters her power
> deep in the blossom of primordial awareness
> and within the thousand-petal lotus
> that floats far above the mind.   RAMPRASAD SEN

Lord Shiva is lying amiably on his back. Ma Kali is standing on his chest, bellowing. They are on a battlefield, and the war is over. Kali struck the final blow. Shiva has been her faithful, though mostly silent, ally. In one of her four hands, her sword is still glistening. She holds the head of a foe in another. She extends her two other hands in a mudra of benediction. One says, "Fear not." The other bestows blessings. Her skin is blue-black, her hair a wild tangle. Her breasts are bare, and her skirt is woven of severed arms.

Kali is the Supreme Mother, and in this legend Shiva is the ground that supports her. Kali's sword cuts through illusion. The head she holds is the mask of ignorance, now free from the bondage of the ego. Her skin is a starless night sky, mysterious passageway from form to formlessness. Her skirt of arms and hands is woven from the karma of her devotees, freely offered.

Kali would do anything for the liberation of her beloved children. And so she smites the enemies of sorrow and delusion. She eats our too muchness and spits out our not enoughness. You are tired of being petty and jealous? Give it to Kali. You really want to wake up? Ask her to awaken you. Irritable and moody? Selfish and sluggish? Kali will relieve you of your burden. Call on her. "Come, Ma. Remove this obstacle and open the way."

But, according to my lifelong friend and mentor, Ram Dass (another feminine mystic in the body of a man), you'd better mean it. Ram Dass received direct transmission of Kali's transformational teachings from his guru, Neem Karoli Baba (Maharaj-ji), in India during the 1960s and '70s. With Maharaj-ji's blessings, Ram Dass brought practices back to the West that synthesized traditional Hindu rituals with contemporary Western spiritual perspectives, in much the same way that classical Theravada Buddhist practices blended with Western psychology to birth the American mindfulness movement.

Whatever you give to Kali, Ram Dass has taught me, she will receive. And if you weren't quite ready, she will come and take it anyway. Her sword will slice you to ribbons. Her fire will turn you to ash. That's how much she loves you. But the opposite is also true: just as the feminine cannot be limited by attributes of gentleness, neither is Kali exclusively fierce. There is an exquisite tenderness in this goddess of liberating change. Fire doesn't only burn; it softens and melts that which is hardened and stuck.

It is important to note that Ma Kali is possibly the most commonly misunderstood and culturally appropriated goddess in the Hindu tradition. We risk cultural appropriation whenever those of us from dominant cultures borrow the symbols and spiritual practices from colonized cultures without fully understanding their context or the depth of their cultural meaning. As we open to Kali, we must resist the impulse to confine her by our small personal ideas and Western gaze.

Emerging from the tradition of West Bengal but finding universal appeal throughout India and beyond, Kali is no less than God Herself. She is the definition of wild mercy and is the unyielding Divine Mother, relentless in her love and spiritual badassness. The iconography of Kali eloquently speaks to the hearts of seekers from many spiritual backgrounds, and she feels suddenly relevant to the Western psyche in our yearning for the feminine during these unmappable, chaotic times.

Anandamayi Ma

> As she played out the *lila* of child, wife, and spiritual guide, she manifested from moment to moment the different aspects of the Mother: the peaceful serenity of Uma, goddess of dawn; the loving delights of Radha, Krishna's playful consort; Kali's protective fierceness; Sita's dharmic perfection; and the mystical energy of Shakti, the manifest cosmos.
>
> RAM DASS, speaking of Anandamayi Ma

When I was sixteen I was pretty sure I'd be enlightened by nineteen, and I was shocked when I still wasn't a fully realized being by twenty-two. Now, in my midfifties, I am being called to teach the dharma, but I am nowhere near where I thought I would be. I still find myself getting caught by some of the booby traps my ego is so skillful at setting for me, such as feeling like I'm never enough and always too much. I am alternately impatient with other people's neuroses and inclined to take things too personally. The separate self is a practical joke I keep falling for.

The image I always held of the perfectly awakened woman was the twentieth-century Indian saint Anandamayi Ma (Bliss-Permeated Mother), who had been roused from the dream of a separate self and left her ego behind. Ma was wild for God.

She frequently fell into ecstatic raptures, and when she wasn't in a trance she was busy dispensing divine wisdom, meeting each pilgrim and devotee exactly where they were along the spectrum of awakening, directly apprehending their souls, and coming up with the perfect solution to their specific spiritual conundrums.

There is nothing wrong (and many things right) about looking to certain great beings as exemplars of states of consciousness to which we aspire. The trouble lies in our pre-conceived notions of what it means to be awake. I will never be Anandamayi Ma. I live in a different time and belong to a different culture than the one that gave rise to that majestic being. But I in my way—just as you are in your way—am already and always an embodiment of divine wisdom. No, I am not equating my neurotic little self with the Divine Mother incarnate. I am identifying here with my true Self, and it is your true Self I am speaking to when I speak to you.

I have come to realize it is not our many imperfections that are the problem but, rather, our ideas of perfection. It's not our attachment to what people think about us that creates suffer-ing but our judgment that there is something wrong with and bad about ourselves. In other words, we are supposed to work, not on being less human, but rather on becoming as fully and deeply human as we can possibly be in any given moment. I can be condescending or needy and still love God with every breath in my body, still be worthy of God's unconditional love. Because, really, I *am* that love. And so are you.

Anandamayi Ma joins my list of subversive women mys-tics I adore. When she had her spontaneous awakening at age twenty-six, following as it did upon years of intensive spiritual practice, she initiated *herself,* simultaneously playing the roles of both guru and disciple. She did not worship one deity to the exclusion of any others, and she engaged religious forms only as a means of transcending form itself. She declined to have sex with her husband, and he became her first and lifelong disciple. Sometimes she was incoherent, weaving her hands in the air in wordless mudras or melting to the floor in a swoon, and other times teachings flowed from her lips in a sublime wisdom stream. She advocated no methods, and she welcomed all beings of every caste and any spiritual tradition. She was iconoclastic yet passionately devoted. She paid no attention to gender and yet was a thoroughly embodied woman.

I guess I still want to be Anandamayi Ma, to speak with clarity and wisdom, and also to throw propriety to the winds. I want to sanction myself and surrender to the One. I want to dissolve, while still being of use in this burning world.

The Poetry of Emptiness

> I carry a torch in one hand and a bucket of water
> in the other:
> With these things I am going to set fire to Heaven
> And put out the flames of Hell
> So that voyagers to God can rip the veils
> And see the real goal.   RABIA

Rabia of Basra was an eighth-century Sufi mystic who escaped captivity to live as a holy hermit in the Arabian Desert. Rabia was born into a desperately poor family and eventually sold into slavery after her parents died. And yet she did not let captivity get in the way of her love affair with the Divine. Consumed with a lifelong desire for a direct encounter with Allah, Rabia managed to pass her days engaged in physical labor and spend all night in prayer.

One night her master awoke to the sound of a cry coming from the roof of his house. Climbing the ladder to investigate, he discovered his servant, Rabia, with her forehead pressed to the ground in submission, calling out to God. She was enfolded by a luminous field that grew brighter the more intensely she prayed. When she lifted her head, sparks seemed to fly from her eyes. The air vibrated with divine Love.

"How could I hold such a being captive?" the master mused. And so, in the morning, he summoned the woman he now recognized as a saint and made her an offer. "Either you can stay here and all the members of my household will serve you as you dedicate your life to prayer, or you may have your freedom and go wherever you wish." Rabia went to the desert.

It's not that Rabia was engaging in some kind of penance or self-mortification to pay for having done something wrong. She wasn't disappearing into the desert for the sake of it. Her life of renunciation was driven by pure and radiant Love. Her only goal was to get out of her own way so that she could get to God.

Rabia was the embodiment of the Sufi path of *fana*, annihilation of the separate self, which leads to *baqa*, divine union. Because she was a brilliant teacher and a sublime poet, Rabia drew the attention of throngs of spiritual seekers who followed her into the desert to sit at her feet. She banished them. Her personal presence was so radiant that many men, often rich and powerful men, wished to marry her. She laughed them off. With a rock as a pillow and a broken jug to carry sometimes water and sometimes food, Rabia roamed the barren landscape praising the One who transcends all naming.

> I exhausted myself, looking.
> No one ever finds this by trying.
> I melted in it and came home,
> Where every jar is full,
> But no one drinks.

At the end of her life, Rabia attained a state of no self, and all her striving dripped into the sands. "What is the secret?" the people wanted to know. "How is it that you have met the Beloved and dwell with him here?" "You know of the how," Rabia said. "I know only the how-less."

deepening

Like so many great mystics, the twentieth-century Indian teacher Ramana Maharshi had a near-death experience that led to spontaneous self-realization. It wasn't illness or injury that brought him to this sacred threshold. It was an experiment in consciousness. He took himself through a process of radical self-inquiry, imagining his own death in detail and paying attention to what it is that remains when what we generally identify with falls away. He realized that we are not our body alone, that we are more than our personality, that there is some abiding spirit that endures, a loving witness, the true Self.

Assume your favorite meditation posture and ask yourself this simple question: "Who am I?" Cultivate your curiosity and open-mindedness. Be willing to peel back the layers of superficial self-definition and go deeper. "I am a woman." *Neti neti* (not this, not that). "I am a mother, a daughter, a lover." *Neti neti.* "I am an activist, an artist, a physician, a baker." *Neti neti.*

You are not denying that you love to make bread or dance your ass off or that you care about carbon emissions or your children's education. What you are doing is lifting the layers of dualistic consciousness and returning to your true, essential, vast, and spacious nature. From this place of luminous emptiness, you can fully engage with your life without being tossed away.

Tears of the Buddha
Gazing on the world below
The goddess is born

CONNECTING

Community and the Web of Interbeing

opening

You feel special. Sometimes this feels like a curse.
Like no one will understand you. Ever. Like you
will always be an alien walking among regular
humans, pretending to blend in. You have learned
to live with this gulf, but what you really crave
is community. You long to belong to the human
family. To Mother Earth.

Participating in the human condition can
be bewildering. It is just not always cozy and
easy—rather, it's humbling at best, downright
humiliating when it's not flowing. It can seem so
much simpler to ride solo, slaying your own dragons
and singing the ballads you wrote about yourself.
Collaboration can be tedious, and the prevailing
masculine value system may have conditioned you
to feel like you are giving away your power when
you share it with others.

So what? Give it away. The time of the singular
sage bestowing his unique wisdom is over. That was
a method devised by the men in charge who sought

to regulate wisdom. They taught us to suffer alone in the desert for forty years, collecting our insights in a secret box labeled "Esoteric Knowledge." Then, we were supposed to dispense those insights stingily to those who proved themselves worthy by also suffering alone for the requisite forty years in the desert.

It turns out that this world is filled with special beings, grappling our way through the anxiety of solitary conundrums and tasting the occasional reprieve of connection. When you realize this, your body lets out its breath and relaxes. The curse lifts. You come in from the cold. You hold out your cup and some other special being fills it with sweet, milky tea spiced with fragrant herbs. You drink.

Our way, the way of the feminine, is to find out what everyone is good at and praise them for it and get them to teach it to one another. Maybe you know something about the hidden meanings of the Hebrew letters, or how to build a sustainable home from recycled tires and rammed soil, or loving-kindness meditation. You, the one who knows the Islamic call to prayer, climb this minaret and call us all to prayer. You, the one who knows how to sit quietly at the bedside of the dying, show us the way to bear witness. You, the one who knows how to get us to wake up to the shadow of privilege, please, wake us the fuck up. It will be chaotic, all this community building, but your cooperation will save the world.

Besides, it will be fun.

We Need Her Voice

When I first began to play with the notion of writing this book, I was animated by optimism about the rising voice of the feminine around the world. Women everywhere were standing up and speaking truth, and the established powers were paying attention. Mainstream values that emphasized money over humanity were shifting, and efforts concerning women and children, refugees and people of color were receiving widespread support. From around the world, people were pouring onto the grounds of the Standing Rock Sioux Reservation to protest the Dakota Access Pipeline and protect the waters, to pray together and offer loving care to Mother Earth.

It seemed clear that patriarchal structures were finally falling out of love with themselves and were looking to the feminine to restore some balance to a polarized paradigm and wholeness to the broken world. Polls indicated a certain win for Hilary Clinton in the 2016 US presidential election. We were about to have the first female president of the United States of America! Like many of my soul sisters, I was puffed up with the certainty that this was our time. I was ready for the feminine to take the stage with a whole new choreography.

Then I went to bed on the eve of the election, and when I woke up in the morning Donald Trump had been elected president of my country. This man was the very embodiment of every value I reject. Having been raised by a feminist mother who modeled self-empowerment, and now being married to a man who is a loving father to multiple daughters and who supports my every aspiration, I had never doubted that I, as a woman, could accomplish any goal and make a meaningful contribution to the world. In contrast, the new president was a misogynist who demeaned women with a breathtaking brashness. I felt like a nuclear bomb had detonated in the night and that it would take years for the full extent of the damage to become evident.

I have always stood in solidarity with the marginalized. The soon-to-be most powerful person on the planet was determined to unravel the social safety net that protected those who lacked access to the spaces and resources disproportionately allotted to the privileged. By virtue of having adopted my children—a decision I made in my youth, when I first confronted the reality of overpopulation and the looming shadow of the climate crisis—mine was a multiracial family. This man was a master of racist rhetoric and an apologist for white supremacy. As a member of the emerging interspiritual movement, my entire life is dedicated to uncovering and sharing the treasures that lie at the heart of the world's religions and spiritual traditions. Donald Trump wanted to ban all Muslims from the shores of our land. Not only was his Islamophobic rhetoric ignorant, it was sacrilegious. Like the proverbial bull in the china shop, he shattered the Golden Rule (treat all beings with the loving-kindness with which you would hope to be treated, or, if you prefer Old King James, "Do unto others as you would have them do unto you" [Matthew 7:12]).

Flabbergasted, heartbroken, I put the proposal for this book aside. The time of the feminine rising was clearly not now, I told myself. I might as well try writing that novel I always thought about. Who wants to listen to me glorifying the vanquished? I would be propping up a corpse and calling her a movie star. I should surrender. We will rise some other time. For now, the emperor was on his throne with his machine gun by his side, and there was not a damn thing we could do about it.

But years of meditation practice have nurtured a modest little witness inside of me who knows better than to believe everything she thinks. As my friend Vera de Chalambert suggested, I turned inward and gave myself permission to not have a clue what was going on or how to make myself useful.

Slowly, I remembered that the feminine mystic is a different creature than the manly prophet. She is not a lone wolf, raising her voice in the wilderness. She is not a strident preacher, warning of doom. She is only as powerful as her community. Alone she is nothing, and she knows it. The very concept of an individual messiah makes no sense to her. When she hears the cries of the world, she reaches out and grasps the hands of her sisters, gathers up her children and asks the blessings of her elders, kisses her lover and turns the kettle to simmer, and rides straight into the arms of the Mystery, where she will wait until it is clear what needs to be done. Then, together with her companions, she will do it.

Look at Mother Mary. A working-class Jewish teenager. Unmarried. She receives an uninvited visit from a vast winged being, who fills her room with his radiance and hands Mary her sacred instructions. "You will be a vessel for the incarnation of the divine here on earth," he declares. "And it's going to hurt like hell to be his mother." Mary trembles, but she stays present. And then she says yes. "*Hineyni.* Here I am. Thy will be done."

That moment between Mary's "no way" and her whole-hearted "yes" is the dark night of the soul. It is a space of numinous mystery, of radical unknowingness. It is unconditional (and usually unintentional) surrender, without a flicker of expectation that everything will be all right. Nothing may ever be okay again, and that's okay. This is the place from which Mary agrees to show up as mother to the whole world. She does not do this alone. She is linked to every mother everywhere, forward and backward in time.

There is a great need to be mothering the world together right now.

So there I sat, an ordinary woman in a slightly apocalyptic world, with a megalomaniacal president, a broken climate, and a signed book contract. I took a breath, wiped the hands of my despair on the jeans of my bodhisattva vow, and renewed my intention to stay present with the pain of the world as long as it would take to ease it. I called on the Shekinah to speak through my written words. I lit a candle and started to write. In between chapters I made soup and answered email and sat at the bedside of a dying friend. I continued to be unskillful in my relationships with my children and a devoted mentor to my students. I found God in all of this. In other words, I got on with the work of the feminine mystic. What else was there to be done? Besides, we need the voice of the feminine more than ever. So I wrote my book.

Building Community

The way of the feminine is the way of connecting. And the path of the mystic leads from the illusion of separation to the reality of divine union, manifested as interdependence with all that is. To walk as a feminine mystic in this world is to recognize that our lives are interpenetrated with the lives of all sentient beings and that the One we love shines from every nexus in that web of interbeing. Whenever we tend to a single strand, we are participating in the care of the whole. When we turn our face from the suffering of any being and walk away, we are exiling ourselves from our Beloved.

Women build community. Not as a mason fabricates a fireplace or a developer plans a shopping mall to maximize consumerism. We create community the way we create a family or a symphony or a good meal: without a lot of grandiosity or demand for accolades. We empower one another. We ask questions, and then we listen, and then we respond. When I lead grief retreats or teach writing workshops—which are largely populated by women—it takes about five minutes before community begins to magically coalesce before my eyes. Without my doing a thing, the people in the room gravitate toward one another and take the risk to trust. They notice one another's wounds and tend them, detect one another's vulnerabilities and protect them, read the stories of one another's souls and affirm them. *How did that happen?* I used to wonder. But I've begun to rely on the invisible force that transmutes a cluster of strangers into a circle of safety. It is the Shekinah in our midst. She comes when we get out of our own way.

I am not, of course, proclaiming that all women are compassionate and relational. I am bewildered about the significant number of my American sisters who vote against their own interests, or claw their way to the top of the corporate ladder at the expense of the most vulnerable, or adopt the very attitudes and strategies of the masculine paradigm that has been used historically to oppress them. And I bow at the feet of my brothers everywhere who willingly abdicate or share their power and join us in getting on with the work of repairing the torn fabric of the world.

Sometimes we drift into despair when we perceive the entrenched power imbalances that devalue life. We cannot imagine how we could possibly rectify anything on our own. The song I am singing—and millions of my sisters and brothers are everywhere echoing the refrain—is one of interdependence and mutual empowerment, of collaboration rooted in love. These are feminine values. Cooperation and emotional connection. Championing one another's efforts to build a better society and supporting one another's projects to sustain the earth.

Recognizing the truth of interbeing, community effortlessly unfolds. This unitive awareness is not reserved for the spiritually adept. We all catch glimpses. Remember those moments of mystical melding, whether in the quietude of contemplative practice or in the rush of awe when we encounter something unspeakably beautiful, when our individual identity melts into the Oneness and sets us free? That's when we recall that there is no separation between ourselves and Ultimate Reality. What we have been seeking has found us and absorbed us into itself. These are fleeting experiences, but they change everything.

Once we have tasted the glory of our unity with all of creation, we can never again fall for the illusion of our independence from the global community. The ego self, the personality we carry around and thrust ahead of us to convince the world of our relevance, becomes irrelevant. And so does the idea of the "other" as an object to be reviled or desired. Donald Trump and the Dalai Lama are both waves on the boundless ocean of being.

This does not mean that the world is a mirage and that our perceptions of pain and injustice are delusional. It means that we have momentarily touched the core of Reality, which is Love, and so it is now incumbent upon us to treat all phenomena as manifestations of that love.

In fact, many of us are already feeling more than ready for horizontal, inclusive leadership. In this more egalitarian and relational dynamic, the insights of particular teachers from various religious traditions are welcomed as worthy contributions offered to and arising from an interconnected community of women. It is accepted that each member of the community, formally trained or not, officially sanctioned by a religious organization or stepping up as a rogue sage, has something of value to offer the whole.

A more feminine flavor of leadership is not something that only women crave. It is nourishment for men as well. Feminine wisdom feeds the human spirit. Mary Magdalene, in her passionate spontaneity, defiance of established plot lines, and the tenderness of her devotion, is an ever-living source of this soul food. Let her nourish you as you step up now. You may look to "the Magdalene" as a role model of an empowered mystic or call upon her as a metaphysical being available as a spirit guide. Either way, she can be an ally in our reclamation of feminine wisdom and power.

INTENTIONAL COMMUNITY

I left home when I was fourteen. This may sound outrageous, but it was 1974 and my family was steeped in the counterculture, where conventional social norms did not apply. Besides, I didn't go far. I moved to the Lama Foundation, an intentional community high in the Sangre de Cristo Mountains around twenty miles from my family's house near Taos, New Mexico. Founded in 1967 by a handful of artists from the East and West Coasts who had the audacity to believe that every one of the world's religions carries a spark of divine truth, the experiment was grounded in the hypothesis that if we gather together and celebrate the sacred through the practices and teachings of all spiritual paths, we can connect with Ultimate Reality and generate peace on Earth. They did not elect a seated leader and did not pay homage to one guru. Nor did they default to a single faith tradition to the exclusion of the others. They invited Zen masters and Sufi sheiks, yogis and yoginis, rabbis and Native American elders, and they harvested the fruits of these ancient lineages. Fifty years later, Lama is still thriving.

Lama's approach to the world's many wisdom ways—with open hands, a listening heart, and a willingness to not have all the answers—strikes me as uniquely feminine. The only leadership position, called the Watch, rotates every two weeks, from new moon to full and back again. Every member of the community, regardless of age or religious education, takes a turn guiding the circle in spiritual practice and welcoming guests. I believe that one of the main reasons the Lama experiment has been so successful is precisely because of this commitment to empowering community and resisting the urge to elect someone to boss everyone else around. It was at Lama that I learned to walk as a feminine mystic in this world.

THE BEGUINES

Intentional community is not a recent phenomenon. The Beguines were a group of women who began gathering in communal households in the Low Countries, primarily the Netherlands and Belgium, in the twelfth century. The last known Beguine died in Ghent in 2014 at the age of ninety-two. Like the Lama Foundation, beguinages were not bound by any strict codes and did not require formal vows. Although their members were Catholic (pretty much the only flavor of religion available to them in Europe during the Middle Ages) and their communities tended toward the monastic, Beguines were not nuns. They were women from across the educational and socioeconomic spectra who chose to dedicate their lives to a balance of interior prayer and service in the world. The Beguines were powerful exemplars of the feminine mystic. They cultivated a direct connection with the Divine in the chambers of their hearts and expressed that intimacy by caring for the poor and sick.

As it turned out, such a choice was a matter of life and death. The church viewed the Beguines with suspicion. Their emphasis on prayer as a private matter between the soul and her God disrupted their institutional hierarchy. These were women who did not require either the permission or the powers of the institutional church to claim their connection to the Divine. Marguerite Porete, probably the most infamous Beguine, was accused of being a "free spirit" and condemned as a heretic.

"I am God, says Love, for Love is God and God is Love, and this soul is God by the condition of Love," Marguerite wrote in her mystical masterpiece, *The Mirror of Simple Souls.* "Thus this precious beloved of mine is taught and guided by me, without herself, for she is transformed into me, and such a perfect one, says love, takes my nourishment." Lover transformed into Beloved? Did she mean the soul is transformed into God? Well, yes. Yes, she did. And she never recanted, either. And so they burned her at the stake.

LOVING YOUR NEIGHBOR

My friend Sister Greta is a Benedictine monastic in the Episcopal tradition who has been deeply formed by the example of the Beguines. For Greta, the essence of the Christian message is one of connection. "Community is so Jesus!" Greta exclaims. "It's at the core of why I am Christian." She reminds me that when Rabbi Jesus was asked what the most important commandment was, he said that we should love God with all our hearts and all our souls and all our strength, and we should love our neighbor as ourselves. "Both of these instructions are utterly and profoundly relational," Greta says. "Loving your neighbor is an obvious way to express connection. But contemplative prayer—silent meditation—isn't about nothingness. It's about sitting in the presence of the Divine. It's about resting in God." It's about Love.

No one could be more surprised than Greta that she turned out to be a Christian, let alone a monastic. Greta was a pioneer in the American yoga movement, cofounding the legendary YogaWorks in Santa Monica, California, and Yoga Zone in New York City. Before that, she was engaged in feminist activism. But while these practices fortified her body and aligned with her values, neither path offered the nourishment Greta's soul hungered for. In 2000, as Greta's carefully woven life was unraveling (marriage, business, housing), a friend encouraged her to do a retreat at an Episcopal monastery in Massachusetts, just to have a chance to breathe and center herself before figuring out her next step.

"On my first day there, an old monk—the kindest person I have ever known—gave me homework," Greta tells me. This assignment was the beginning of her "conversion experience." He instructed her to go back to her room that evening and sit across from an empty chair and imagine Jesus sitting in it. "Unburden your heart," the monk directed Greta. "Tell him everything." Greta shared the depths of her pain with the imaginary Jesus. She wept her way through the entire exercise. "And I felt nothing in return," Greta admits.

But later that night, when Greta finally lay down to sleep, she became suddenly and intensely aware of a vast presence—not a personal Jesus, but the Cosmic Christ. It did not have a body, but rather was composed of a kind of electrified light. Greta half sat up and was held in place by this electric light streaming back and forth between Greta's heart and the heart of the Cosmic Christ. She felt (rather than heard) the words: "First we must heal your heart." Then she lay back down and sensed all her sorrow draining away. In that moment, she knew she was healed. After that, Greta simplified her life, giving away almost everything she owned and paring all her belongings down to what would fit in a single room, which is how she has lived ever since.

"I just knew I wanted to live as a monastic," Greta tells me. "I wanted my whole life to be about God." She began seeking an intentional spiritual community to match her longing for a life of prayer and service. "I had asked God what she wanted me to do for her and she led me to the word *chaplain*. Then I met Dennis, who was a chaplain in the jails, and I knew this was what I was supposed to be doing." It turns out Dennis, too, had a monastic calling, and so together they created the Community of Divine Love in Southern California.

Brother Dennis and Sister Greta balance their days between praying the Divine Office—the five contemplative prayers in the Benedictine tradition—and ministering to human beings caught up in the toxic web of the Los Angeles prison system. Whenever I visit the Community of Divine Love I am struck by the joy that radiates from the hearts of these gentle monks and can imagine how it oozes like light through the shadowed passageways of the jails and prisons where they spend most days, healing and transfiguring every heart they encounter.

It may no longer be deadly to form small communities dedicated to the values of contemplative practice and environmental sustainability, but it's still subversive. Living with other human beings is one of the most challenging things most of us will ever do. It's hard enough to coexist with our own partners and children. Making decisions and making meals and making a difference in the world in conjunction with a bunch of people who used to be strangers requires a depth of surrender and humility rarely demanded of us in mainstream Western society.

If we look to the feminine, drawing on the innate value of relationship, we can navigate these alternative social structures and find a viable path through the changes that are coming. We do not need to reside in intentional communities like Lama Foundation or a beguinage to live lovingly and responsibly as feminine mystics, but it's vital in these times of desperate divisiveness that we reach out to the rest of the human family and affirm the truth of our interconnection in any and every way that we can.

The Feminine Prophet

Not every mystic is naturally prophetic, and not every prophet leans toward the mystical. Traditionally, the primary concern of the mystic has been communion with the Divine, and the major issue for the prophet has been speaking truth. For the feminine, however, the line between contemplative life and social and environmental action is blurry to the point of insignificance. She turns inward, where she recognizes herself in all beings, which moves her to turn outward and act on behalf of the whole.

All times are urgent times, yet I don't think humanity as a whole has ever faced the magnitude of the threat of imminent extinction with which we are presently confronted. And rather than doing everything they can to thwart disaster, certain men in charge of steering the ship of the world are leading us straight into the iceberg.

We need all hands on deck. While it is not in everyone's nature to vocally decry the violation of human rights and the degradation of the planet, I believe that we are all on some level prophets, women and men, and that all prophets are reluctant prophets. At least the real ones are. We stammer and protest when we are called upon to stand up and do something about the suffering around us. We cannot imagine how the Holy One could have picked us to speak through when there must be so many more worthy mouthpieces to choose from. If I were God (which I am, and which you are, too) and someone was applying for the job of prophet, I would send him away at once. I would mistrust his motivation.

Look at Hildegard of Bingen, the medieval Rhineland visionary: a true prophet. Hildegard starts having visions of the being who calls itself the Living Light when she is a small child. Her prophecies so deeply disturb the adults that she wrestles the messages down and plows them under. She buries them as a girl and stuffs them back down as a woman whenever they begin to rise again. But they continue to smolder in the subterranean zone of her soul, threatening to destroy her if she does not share them.

At last, on the threshold of death, she gives in. She sits up and starts writing down the cosmological information that comes coursing through her. Her illness falls away. She writes and she draws, she composes heavenly chorales and she concocts healing remedies. She praises the Divine Mother—Mary, Sophia, the Earth—and invites us all into intimate relationship with the vital essence flowing through all of creation.

Look at Fatima, daughter of the Prophet Muhammad, whose name means "Resplendent One." Those who knew Fatima, from the time she was a little girl until her death at age twenty-nine, remarked on the luminosity of her countenance. Many feel that it was Fatima who was meant to carry the Prophet's lineage. Muhammad did not have the opportunity to name his successor before he died. This ambiguity created the historic rift among Muslims commonly referred to as the Sunni/Shi'a split. Some of his followers felt the Prophet would have wanted the community to decide among themselves who would succeed him after his death (Sunni). Others thought that Ali, who was both Muhammad's cousin and his son-in-law, should lead the community (Shi'a).

But there is ample evidence that Muhammad revered his daughter Fatima more highly than any other woman, placing her as equal in status to Mary, who is so profoundly respected in Islam that an entire chapter of the Holy Qur'an is dedicated to her. It seems entirely possible to many people, Muslim and non-Muslim, that Fatima was the most qualified of all potential successors. We have not heard whether or not Fatima clamored for this position or even imagined herself worthy. She simply continued to love Allah with all her heart and all her soul and all her strength and to be of comfort to those who suffered. She suffered terribly herself.

This must be how it feels to be a prophet: we are swallowed up, like the biblical prophet Jonah in the belly of the great fish, and must spend some time suspended in the darkness. We agree to be a spokesperson for God and then, as happened to Muhammad, bearing that burden almost crushes us. We get our people through the narrow straits of Egypt, like Moses and his siblings Miriam and Aaron did, only to discover that our people seem to prefer the comfortable misery of slavery. Like Mother Mary and Mary Magdalene, we love the Beloved against all odds and through all consequences.

Tears of the Buddha

One day Avalokiteshvara, the Buddha of compassion, stood on the mountaintop gazing down into the valley where human beings were busy with their work of suffering. They burned and moaned, reached out and drew back, were born and died and were reborn to do it all again. He couldn't bear it. His eyes filled with tears, and he wept. One of these tears crystallized into Tara, the bodhisattva of compassion. She stood up, looked around, and spontaneously she vowed: "I will strive for the liberation of all beings for as long as beings exist. And I will do this always as a woman." And then she sat down to meditate for ten million years, during which time tens of millions of beings were set free by the power of her practice.

This is the feminine version of the bodhisattva vow. It may sound like a grave matter, but it is not solemn. Tara is playful, irreverent, and wild in her mercy. When we begin to take ourselves and our spiritual path too seriously, Tara shows up to play tricks on us and get us to laugh at our own self-righteousness. She pulls the rug out from under those who show disrespect for the feminine. On the field of the open mind, Tara dances. In the sea of the open heart, Tara soothes all wounds. She has eyes on the palms of her hands and the soles of her feet. Seeing the pain of the world and acting with compassion are integrated realities.

Tara helps us to remember: We are not on our own. There are countless women hearing the call, extending their hands, blessing and strengthening us to step up. We cannot and should not transmute the toxins of the prevailing paradigm inside the cells of our own individual bodies. The alchemy happens in a circle. We need to weave together our threads of care and transfigure this tapestry. It is only together that we can reimagine the territorial treaty we've inherited as a generous invitation to a communal feast. Look around. Your allies are everywhere. And they love you.

deepening

Mystical Jewish wisdom teaches us that we are all born with a particular task we are meant to do to contribute to the healing of the world, and we are precisely and perfectly designed to do it. What is the unique task imprinted on your soul? Hint: it is probably something you are already good at and is almost definitely something you love doing.

Sit quietly, with your eyes closed (or downward cast and unfocused). Allow yourself

to contemplate your strengths and imagine
how you might harness them for the benefit of
others. Write down a list of ways you could rise
to the call, even if they don't look like dramatic
contributions or if they take a very different
form than you might have imagined. Be wildly
creative. Make a plan of action to implement
one of these ideas.

Skin meets skin and sings
Two become one becomes two
Most sacred embrace

6

EMBRACING

Sexual Embodiment

opening

You have experienced your body and your lover's body
as instruments, perfectly designed to play the music
of the Beloved. This has at times impelled you to
foist all your devotional impulses onto your intimate
partners. Sometimes they appreciated it, but most
of the time they didn't even notice, or else it made
them uncomfortable. You confused depressed bass
players with Krishna. You tried to make pompous
professors into the Lord of Love. You thought your
attraction to other women would save you. They were
all distractions. The radiance of the real thing was too
much to bear.

Once you began to suspect that your adoration was
misplaced, you shifted your quest from the bars and the
ashrams to the innermost chamber of your own soul.
And there (lo and behold) was the Beloved, reclining
on a sumptuous bower pouring wine (naked). "It's you!"
(cried you) and you leapt into the Beloved's arms (who
laughed and covered you with kisses). It was clear the
Beloved had been waiting (patiently) for a long time.

You exchanged marriage vows with the Beloved, disguised as a vow of celibacy. *If I can just break my addiction to relationships*, you reasoned, *I can get on with loving God.* For a time this promise proved promising. Then it began to fossilize. You were holding on to a notion, once a nourishing truth, and it was turning to ash in your hands. The bliss of union with the One had deteriorated into a dualistic pronouncement. Human lovers: illusory. The Divine Within: the only thing that's real. Sexlessness seemed safe. By firing the men and women you once loved, you could avoid working out the messy particulars of the experience of incarnation, wherein your heart gets broken and your ego gets transfigured.

One day, along came someone who also loved the Beloved. And they loved you, too.

They did not love you instead of the Beloved. They loved you because they saw the eyes of the Beloved shining behind your tears. They tasted the fragrance of the Beloved between your thighs. They pondered the sacred scripture of your conversations over coffee in the mornings or wine at sunset. They claimed your relationship as the landscape where the Holy One dwells. Surprise! Their love freed you to love the Beloved. Safe in the sanctuary of their embrace, you grew strong enough to cultivate a direct connection with the sacred. You are not an obstacle, it turns out. You are the passageway from separation to union.

Now that you are well loved by a good man or a good woman, you can carry on a torrid dalliance with the Beloved. And your partner is strong enough not to mind this affair one bit. In fact, it makes them love you all the more. What is more alluring than a woman enflamed by desire for the Holy One?

Holy Desire

All desire is holy desire. At least its roots are. Sometimes the pure flower of wanting withers and turns toxic. That's when all kinds of aberrations and addictions start cropping up and ruining things. But the original impulse springs from love. And all love is One Love. Love is the nature of the universe.

Organized religion has desecrated the sacred altar of desire. This probably has a lot to do with the fact that men run the religious show and that they are petrified of wanting women (or other men) too much. How can they be in control of the universe when their hearts and loins are being stirred up with feelings that upset the carefully constructed and meticulously ordered structures they've erected (pun intended)? Religion is tidy—and therefore dependable. Sex is unpredictable—and therefore dangerous.

In every one of the world's major spiritual traditions, we can see where men in power took a perfectly reasonable boundary and turned it into a scary sin. For example, it seems like a great idea to rein in a young man—whose hormones tend to run amok—for a spell, by means of a temporary commitment to celibacy. It's like fasting: it flushes the systems and clarifies the perspective.

But it would be counterproductive to spend one's entire life starving. A lifelong vow of celibacy may work fine for some people, but for others it represses wholesome desires by shoving them into the dark, where they fester into a range of unhealthy behaviors, from overeating to child abuse. This is the type of trouble that's plagued the Catholic Church, where clergy are required to take a lifetime vow of celibacy. It is not only the Roman Catholic tradition that glorifies renunciation. Many Hindu and Buddhist monastic communities also require vows of chastity, informed by the belief that sex, if unrestrained, could lead to a breakdown of the social fabric and distract the monks from their interior life. I get it. Abstinence has its spiritual function. But forever?

What would sexuality look like if, instead of forbidding people to have sex with each other (or themselves), we encouraged mindfulness in all our sensual experiences? What happens when, as we caress our lover's belly, we become intentionally curious about every nuance of the contact between our fingers and their skin? What about when our lover treats the curve of our clavicle and the rising of our nipples with complete attention? The power of presence softens the lines between self and other. This is what the Jewish philosopher Martin Buber meant by an "I-Thou" relationship. When we deeply connect with another being, we touch the Divine. It is difficult to objectify and abuse someone with whom you are fully present and in whose face you behold the face of God.

The Shadow

Of course, desire has its dark side. When I was a teenager, I hooked up with a much older guy (a.k.a. "the charlatan master") who lavished me with more attention than I had ever received in my life. I was beautiful! I was brilliant! And practically an enlightened being! Not only did he make me feel special, but he made me feel safe and protected. Coming from an offbeat upbringing that involved a large dose of chaos and uncertainty, the constancy of his care was a cave in which I took refuge.

It's also where we hid. Something in my soul knew the intimacy was wrong. I remember one night at a farm in Mendocino, California, where we had a caretaking gig. We had been washing dishes in the kitchen after dinner and it was late. To get back to the cabin in the woods where we were staying with a few friends, we had to pass through a dense redwood forest. It was so dark I could not see him beside me, but I could feel him. I could hear his footfalls and smell his unwashed hair.

Suddenly, an ominous feeling came over me. The hairs on my arms rose, and a chill ran down my spine. I felt that I was in the presence of true evil, and every muscle in my body was poised to bolt. "This is ridiculous," I chided myself. "This is your beloved. He is a saint (he told you so himself). Get a grip." I forced myself to dismiss the creepy feeling as an artifact of my unruly imagination. Or maybe, I argued to myself, what was happening was that the forces of darkness were trying to blot out the light that was being generated by our sacred love.

By this point we had been having illicit sex for about a year. I had grown to depend on his affection and could not bear the thought of being without him. And so I stuffed that warning signal under the covers of my heart, and whenever I detected the flashing red light through the layers of denial, I rationalized it away.

I recall another time when I knew that I was snared in a toxic web with this man. We were camping alone in the desert of Canyonlands National Park. One day we decided to drop acid. Now, I should let you know here that I was terrified of drugs, having had LSD slipped to me when I was thirteen, which, as I mentioned earlier, precipitated years of flashbacks and dissociative states. But my lover convinced me that tripping in this beautiful environment with my valiant protector to guide me would be not only safe but also liberating.

It was neither safe nor liberating. As the effects of the drug crashed over me, I perceived my beloved as the devil. I didn't even believe in such a creature, but in that moment this man, my intimate, embodied every fantasy image of Satan. He was foul and cruel, despotic and pathetic. And he wanted to consume my soul. If I could have fled I would have, but there was nowhere to go. And so I perched on a slab of sandstone beside him and silently waited out the voyage through hell. Eventually we got up and drove slowly through the campground, listening to Dire Straits on the car stereo, which calmed me a little, and when the sun began to set, splashing the desert with fractured light, we scrambled some eggs, fried some bacon, and drank beer. The Evil One faded. My man lit the Coleman lantern and read me another chapter from *Autobiography of a Yogi*.

There is a balance women must strike between dropping the sexual constraints imposed on us by several millennia of patriarchal oppression and maintaining boundaries grounded in self-care. On the one hand, we are calling out men who have used positions of privilege and power to molest and demean women, demanding they wake up to their unconscious misogyny and take responsibility for their hurtful actions. On the other hand, we are claiming ownership of our own desires and celebrating the freedom to fully inhabit our bodies and enjoy our interaction with other free bodies. This dance of conscious intimacy is one of the most sacred practices available to us and one of the most daring.

DIVINE DYSMORPHIA

Women know. Our bodies know. Our souls know. We are blessed and cursed with the ability to sense malevolence. We can tell when we are unsafe, when we are being violated. Even though I was raised by feminist parents and came of age in a society that was much better at empowering women than it had ever been, I was still heir to certain cultural throwbacks that encouraged me to stuff my knowing in favor of being taken care of. The charlatan—this man who secretly slept with me while I was a teenager and whom I later married—was my life. If I were to leave him, he assured me, the integrity of the universe would come undone. I left. And sure enough, when I left it all unraveled. I hurtled through the universe . . . and landed in the center of my own being.

Yet, while I am now so intimate with my own core that I am unlikely to stray far, I still waver. I still find myself subtly seeking the approval of men, and something in me relaxes when I get it. I still buy into society's standards of feminine beauty. I confess to being overly concerned with my body mass index. I can (and do) look at women who are much heavier than I am with appreciation of their beauty. I find their soft curves sexy. But I strive for a jutting clavicle, an angular pelvis, a concave belly in myself. I count every calorie I consume, reflexively tallying them at the end of each day. I compulsively exercise, eager to make up lost days at the gym. Whenever my jeans become a little tight, my self-worth begins to deflate.

It embarrasses me to admit this, and yet it would be disingenuous to pretend that just because I am writing this book on feminine wisdom, I am wise about all the ways I may have internalized five thousand years of values that benefited men over women. I long ago realized that my eating issues are less about aesthetics than they are about power. I'm not trying to win a swimsuit competition. I am trying to muscle in a place at the table with the big boys. If only my hips were straight and my chest flat, I could pass as a guy! Then I would not have to apologize for my existence, for my passion and my opinions.

I am a woman with curves. Even if I were to starve myself (which I tried throughout my twenties) I would still have wide hips and full breasts. My thighs would still be thick, and my ass would still be rounded. So this antifat crusade is an exercise in futility. I am not suggesting that women simply capitulate and abandon all efforts to be healthy and fit. Tending the vessel of this body is a sacred act. Eating clean, healthy foods and engaging in physical exertion are forms of prayer. But I am not always clear on the difference between self-care and body dysmorphia. I don't always know if I am watching what I eat and lifting weights out of liberated self-love or unconscious self-hatred. I'm working on this. It's hard to see our own shadow; it straggles in our wake.

What I strive to remember is that it is a worthy practice, a holy path, to honor and celebrate the body. And not just the limited ideals of the body imposed upon us by men (and unconsciously upheld by women who judge themselves and each other as not measuring up to the impossible standards of the fashion and beauty industries). The awakened woman honors every shape and size and hue of the physical form. The Divine Feminine is a prism who throws her radiant reflections in all directions. She is prepubescent, and she is ancient. She is lithe, and she is voluptuous. She is rich brown and she is opalescent. She has two breasts or one or none. She is sighted or blind, in robust health or grappling with a terminal diagnosis. She is gorgeous and perfect. She is desirable, and her desires are worthy. Her desires are holy. To desire her is to be blessed.

THE MIDDLE WAY

When the Buddha arose from his long *samadhi* (deep state of meditation) under the bodhi tree, his first discourse was about the Middle Way. He was advocating for a balance between excessive self-indulgence and radical asceticism. He preached the four noble truths in an effort to point out the road to true happiness. The first truth the Buddha identified is that existence is predicated on suffering, or *dukkha*, which has also, and more expansively, been translated as "unsatisfactoriness." The second truth is that suffering has a cause, and the cause is *tanha*, "desire" or "craving." The third truth is that we can reduce suffering by letting go of desire. And the fourth truth is that there is a remedy for this syndrome: the eightfold path, which consists of right views, right intention, right speech, right conduct, right livelihood, right effort, right mindfulness, and right meditation.

The glitch originates with a fundamental misunderstanding of the Pali word tanha. If we simply translate it as "desire" we are likely to pathologize a perfectly natural and impossible-to-eradicate attribute of the human condition. Many people have ended up using this "truth" as an excuse to beat the shit out of themselves and each other on the grounds that it must be unspiritual to fancy a good cuddle or a chocolate brownie sundae (with coffee ice cream, thank you).

I have a feeling this was the opposite of what the Buddha meant for us to take away from his famous Deer Park Sutra, his first sermon following his awakening. I believe that what the Buddha meant (and plenty of people agree with me here, like the American-born teacher of Tibetan Buddhism Pema Chödrön, who expresses this more artfully than I ever could) was something like this: When we can allow things to be just what they are and show up for reality with open hands, clear eyes, and a compassionate heart, a space opens in which there is room for both the fire of desire and also equanimity. We can want without clinging. We can release without pushing away. And when we surrender to reality, reality doesn't hurt as much.

The way of the feminine is about neither repressing nor indulging. Well, maybe it's a tad indulgent, since it's about reclaiming the holiness of passion, blessing the burning of yearning, saying yes to the wild, untamed, unrestrained dance of life. It's more about celebrating the holy sweetness of the body: sex, food, exercise, rest.

Reimagining the Mary Magdalene Archetype

In *Dark Night of the Soul,* John of the Cross describes Mary Magdalene's passion for Jesus as symbolic of the birthright of the human soul so on fire for God that she will do whatever is necessary to get to her Beloved. Mary storms the halls of the rich and powerful, demanding to see her Beloved, and when she finds him dining with the dudes she cracks open a bottle of priceless nard (an aromatic oil) and washes his feet with it. Then she dries each foot with her hair. Is Jesus mortified that his female disciple would show up uninvited in an exclusive male space? Nope. Is he horrified that she would squander such an expensive substance? He is not. Does he tell her she does not belong? He doesn't. Instead, he praises her for her love and uplifts her as an example to us all.

In Hinduism, the feet of the guru are incomparably holy. To touch the dust of the Beloved's lotus feet symbolizes the relationship between teacher and disciple. There is another biblical story in which the Magdalene washes her Beloved's feet with her tears. She is watering the lotus feet of the guru from the wellspring of her love and her pain, and the Beloved blooms for her and for all beings!

As it turns out, the woman in the Gospels who washes Jesus's feet and dries them with her hair may not have been Mary Magdalene at all. Recent scholarship suggests that conflating an unknown female "sinner" with Mary Magdalene may have been a way the early Roman church attempted to marginalize and discount her power and influence on Jesus's life. Mary was, in fact, a woman of means, and a close companion of Jesus, on whose resources the young Rabbi Jesus and his immediate followers seemed to depend. The church has continued to minimize Mary Magdalene's legitimacy ever since and to use her as an excuse to denigrate women and bar them from positions of religious authority.

Not only was Mary Magdalene an apostle in her own right, but she was probably the Apostle of the Apostles, a status officially conferred upon her by Pope Francis at the late date of 2016! The Magdalene was present at the foot of the cross as Jesus suffered and died, present at his burial, present to anoint his body the morning after Shabbat, when he first revealed his resurrected self and sent her off to spread the good news of his deathlessness to the rest of the disciples. It was around six hundred years later, during the rule of Pope Gregory I, that Mary Magdalene was relegated to the status of repentant prostitute. From then on, her mastery was (intentionally) blotted out.

Was there more to Jesus and Mary Magdalene's relationship than master and disciple or even religious colleagues? Probably. It seems unlikely that a young Jewish man in first-century Palestine would have been unmarried, no matter how countercultural his lifestyle may have been. It is with good reason that the literary imagination has been captivated by the question of whether or not Mary Magdalene and Jesus of Nazareth were lovers and whether they may have conceived a child together. To me, these questions are not unlike the issue of the virginity of Mary, mother of Jesus. Did Mother Mary really get pregnant without having sex, or was her "virginity" more a matter of the purity of her surrender to God?

These are intriguing speculations, yet potentially misleading. The sexual facts of the matter can distract us from what is an even more subversive question: Why did the Christian community fail to acknowledge Mary Magdalene as the intimate spiritual companion—probably closest disciple, maybe even spiritual equal—to Rabbi Jesus? And how has this mischaracterization of Mary Magdalene excluded women from full participation in Christ's lineage? Mary's way was the way of the heart. She exemplified devotion. The institutionalized church is the way of the analytical mind. Mary's teachings are rooted in the body and grounded in direct experience with the sacred. The dogma of the church demanded unquestioned adherence to established doctrines and prescribed rituals. Given her personal relationship with Christ—a connection that did not require the intercession of a male authority figure—it isn't difficult to see why Mary Magdalene would be perceived as a threat.

NEITHER MADONNA NOR WHORE

Our postmodern world is starting to recover from the Madonna and whore dichotomy bequeathed to us by the Roman church, in which our only choices as women were to either serve as loyal (read: chaste, boring) wives or dwell at the fringes of society as dirty and defiled (yet irresistible) prostitutes. We have developed a more nuanced view of female sexuality and have mostly dismissed chastity as an arcane and counterproductive concept (though it creeps into the culture in all kinds of insidious ways, leading women and girls to question our own worth when we ought to be cherishing ourselves).

Contemporary Western women have begun to recognize that we have options in this life beyond pleasing men and bearing their babies. Increasingly, men are no longer as conditioned to put their wives out to pasture, sexually speaking, after we have raised their children or to treat their spouses as their mothers once they are partnered up. Such things still happen, of course, but heightened awareness about the fullness of a woman's personhood makes it a little harder to hide. Although our consumerist society continues to objectify young women, the cultural conversation is shifting to awaken men's consciousness around safety, consent, and the inherent dignity of female bodies. At least white bodies. Black and brown women are still both publicly policed in ways no white woman would be and also disproportionately subject to acts of sexualized violence in staggering (and largely underreported in the white-dominated mainstream press) numbers.

Women have reached a tipping point all over the globe, refusing to be disrespected for another minute. From Hollywood to Washington, DC, from India to Mexico, inside our churches and within our extended families, we are coming together to support one another in redressing the harms incurred as a result of the age-old sanction of sexual abuse. Those of us with the privilege to express our anger without fearing for our lives are engaging in fierce truth telling, defying all the unspoken rules that make us pay for speaking out.

We haven't made as much headway when it comes to women's power as we have with women's sexuality. We still seem to expect our female political leaders to be tough and shrewd, and then we blame them for being "too masculine." In the spiritual arena, women who become leaders often capitulate to the masculine prerogative, earning titles and amassing followers who then assign these women a kind of elevated status that sets them apart. While women's access to seminaries and our ability to be ordained is a cause for celebration, female rabbis, roshis, priests, and swamis often unconsciously recreate the very structures feminism seeks to dismantle. They issue commands, demand obedience, and preside over rituals reserved for elite religious officials, effectively barring anyone who is not formally sanctioned from sharing spiritual gifts of their own.

Sacred Spectrum

Embodied feminine spirituality is not confined to the domain of those who identify as female. Just as rigid religious affiliation is evolving before our eyes into recognition of the living truth at the heart of all spiritual traditions, so too does a more fluid relationship with sexual identity liberate us to cultivate a direct and authentic connection with the sacred. Many First Nations peoples have recognized for millennia that some individuals are gifted with both a male and a female soul, which endows them with the ability and the responsibility to serve as healers for their communities.

My friend Kishan is a sun dancer in the Lakota tradition. They have also been a nonbinary person for as long as they can remember ("they" is the pronoun many nonbinary people prefer). Originally from Trinidad, Kishan carries their Afro-Caribbean roots into their Lakota life. My friend is a contemplative activist who spends long hours in silence and stillness every day and is also engaged in social justice issues in Albuquerque, where they also live.

One day, in meditation, Kishan was told that they must go on a solitary vision quest on ceremonial land, dragging the sacred buffalo skull tethered to their pierced back, and that they must do this on behalf of the Divine Feminine. Like any respectable prophet, Kishan second-guessed the divine summons, and then gave in.

In the midst of their solitary agony, Kishan had a vision of Jesus. They understood that Jesus was there to share their suffering and that they were never really alone, that no one is ever truly alone. The masculine model of suffering alone for the sake of spiritual development has no place in the sacred heart of the Christ. Jesus was helping Kishan to carry their cross, to bear the buffalo skull, to receive a healing vision, to dance to the sun for the Divine Feminine.

Jesus coming to the aid of a dark-skinned nonbinary sun dancer from the Caribbean who carries a buffalo skull in honor of the Divine Feminine? Yes! Kishan is not the only person I know who is challenging existing stereotypes of feminine spirituality. One of the most gifted philosophy students I ever had the honor to teach, the child of a Jewish mom and a Chicano dad, not only transitioned from male to female but also converted to Islam, upending half a dozen cultural assumptions about what it is to be a woman on a path of spiritual awakening (combined, by the way, with a committed practice of social justice). And then there's Billy, a transgender man who used to be a neo-pagan feminist named Annie. Billy told me that when he was a member of an exclusively female Wiccan group, he spent a lot of energy trying to embody the Goddess. This never felt quite right. Now that he's a man, Billy revels in being the consort of the Goddess, rather than trying to be the Goddess. If anything, he says, he has begun to embody Pan, the horned god, who loves and protects the Goddess and all her children.

More and more children in Western society seem to be entering adulthood with an expansive sense of their own gender identity. I see this expressed in the classrooms where I teach and filling the horizons of every social media platform. These youth approach sexuality with an open heart and a curious mind, ready to love whom they love, without the burden of preconceived gender roles to limit their encounter with the beauty of the other. This spaciousness gives me hope for a more peaceful world, one in which it is the heart that leads the way.

The Divine Masculine

Sometimes guys challenge people like me: "Hey, why don't you ever talk about the Divine Masculine?"

I have a couple of responses. One is: "Because thousands of years of male domination have sort of thrown the world out of balance, and this conversation about the Divine Feminine is an effort to rectify that a bit."

My other response is: "I have no idea what that even looks like."

Then I remember to take off my armor and allow myself to feel what the Divine Masculine looks like in my heart. And I realize it looks like my husband, Ganga Das (a.k.a. Jeff). And my brother, Roy. And my dear friend, a Roman Catholic priest and iconographer whom I affectionately call Father Billy. And at least a dozen other men I know and love (or admire from afar).

My husband embodies that mythical blend of manly man and nurturer. When we first got together, Ganga Das had three daughters of his own, and I brought two more into the mix. The man ended up with five daughters! And a couple of wives. Well, not at the same time. In fact, there was a respectable gap between us, during which he engaged in the rigors of shadow work—at first through attending a group or two, then by reading books like *Iron John* and *Codependent No More*, and ultimately by turning fully inward to face himself with curiosity and courage. By the time I got him, he was deliciously seasoned and ready to step up as a divine dude.

Ganga Das does all those things men have been conditioned to do for women. He fixes broken stuff, navigates us through cities and wildernesses, whacks the weeds with his gas-powered weed whacker, grills chicken on the barbecue, and lights the pilot of the radiant floor system at the end of October. I cannot tell you how much I appreciate all of these tasks, how I rest in them.

He also prepares the perfect cup of tea with milk and honey and presents it to me with a gallant flourish. He listens to the same litany of self-doubts—ever newly reimagined—while we're soaking together in the tub. He thinks I'm smart and also wise, and he finds a way to mention this almost every day. Whenever I take off my clothes he gasps as if I were Venus stepping off the half shell and into his arms, even though we have been together for a couple of decades and I'm showing signs of wear and tear by now. When I have some new accomplishment he celebrates me, and when I am disappointed he comforts me, and when I am sick he tends me. But he does not overdo the praising or the commiserating or the nursing. His care is grounded in dignity—both his own and mine.

In case you are currently turning green with envy, let me just say that the other thing that makes my husband a reliable example of the Divine Masculine is his very human collection of flaws. Ganga Das is a Vietnam veteran, and he is not all that connected to his emotions. He can be very supportive to others in distress, but he rarely allows himself to fully feel his own feelings. The only times I have ever seen him cry were for about thirty seconds when his father died and maybe another half a minute when my daughter died. It was not as if he didn't love these two people with all his heart. He did. And he mourned them. But something in his psyche has been quashed by a combination of his middle-class American upbringing, being drafted as a young surfer into the army and shipped off to Southeast Asia, and subsequent years of living in an ashram engaging in rigorous *sadhana* (spiritual practice). As a result he does not do well with messy feelings. Instead, he makes jokes. He is very funny. This playful spirit has gotten him far—and also far away. I live with this paradox. So does he. It does not trouble me.

So what does the Divine Masculine look like as it's walking this earth? It looks like men who can make fun of themselves, laughing at the great cosmic joke happening in the form of their own lives, and cracking up the rest of us with their irreverent holy wit. It also looks like kindness. Cascades of loving-kindness, freely offered, without a trace of entitlement. Like Hanuman, the monkey god in the Hindu tradition, whose saintliness is intertwined with his thinking that he's nothing special, the men I perceive as the most luminous examples of the Divine Masculine would never, ever agree with me about their divinity. They think they're just monkeys.

Phases of Life

Our relationships with ourselves and each other morph as we mature. Change is built into our bodies. Hormones influence the shape of our desires. Wisdom grows even as fecundity diminishes. What once drove us begins to slow down enough to let us hop off and amble. We start to notice the ubiquitous beauty that we had been too distracted to notice. We come home to our own dear bodies in ways we never could have experienced when we were in full flower. What used to matter doesn't so much, and new things become important. We are developmentally designed to accept these changes, even if we are culturally conditioned to resist them. Sometimes our most profound spiritual experiences unfold after middle age.

My friend Gangaji offers a powerful example of the way our inner lives can shift as we age, bringing us into closer contact with our embodied experience. After a lifetime of seeking, this contemporary American spiritual teacher had an awakening at the age of forty-eight, when she met her own teacher and all her striving for things to be different than they were fell away. As I pointed out to Gangaji, this is the same age that Teresa of Ávila was when she had what is referred to as her "second conversion," in which she spontaneously realized that her heart had been closed to the truth of love that had been with her all along in the form of Christ and would be present forevermore. For both Gangaji and Teresa, direct connection to the simple truth of What Is changed everything. Up to that point, both women had expended an enormous amount of energy trying to meditate their way through the problem of being human.

"I remember sitting on the curb as an eleven-year-old girl in Mississippi trying to figure out how to get out of here," Gangaji told me. By "here" she meant the full range of impediments imposed by her restrictive Southern life. Conditioned to believe that the right man would save her, the young Gangaji learned to use men as an escape. Sexual bliss, like ever-deepening states of meditation, succeeded in providing temporary relief from her human suffering, but true serenity eluded her until she met the Indian holy man Papaji. That's when she discovered that "what we perceive to be in the way is the way." She let go. She relaxed. And peace (and a good sense of humor and a big dose of loving-kindness) came flooding into the space that had been taken up by all that effort.

As we spoke about this, Gangaji had an epiphany. She was eleven when she started her quest, the same year she had her first period. She was forty-eight when her quest ended with meeting Papaji, which happened to coincide with the beginning of her menopause. Many of the experiences of those middle years—both the sexual and the spiritual—were at least partially informed by biochemistry, as they are for most women.

As the hormones began to flow, young Toni (renamed Gangaji by Papaji after he became her teacher) was swept into a dance of desire and discipline that unfolded over the course of the next four decades. These experiences carried her to great heights of bliss and deep desert spaces. As her physical reality shifted in midlife, her soul was able to naturally access the sweet ease she had always sought through spiritual practice. Gangaji laughed in delight as this realization unfurled.

We made the connection between Gangaji's experience and the Hindu teaching of the "phases of life." Hinduism, one of the most inclusive and accepting of all spiritual traditions, recognizes that human life tends to follow a certain trajectory. The "student" phase begins with puberty. This is when we hunger to learn all we can about life. We may sit at the feet of a teacher, absorbing all the knowledge and wisdom we can take in. In our midtwenties, most of us answer the call to partner up. This is known as the "householder" phase. We start families and engage with our communities. It is a time that is characterized by duty. In middle age, traditionally marked by the birth of the first grandchild, we return our attention to the inner life. This is the "retirement" phase. We may leave the comfort and security of home and set out on a new quest, very different from the adventure seeking of our youth, informed now by a lifetime of suffering and sweetness, of mistakes and breakthroughs. In old age, we return home, no longer driven by the need to gain spiritual wisdom. Instead, we radiate wisdom by simply being. Such a luminous elder is called a "sannyasin."

Many of the women I know are in the retirement phase. This does not imply that they play golf all day or travel around in their RVs (though spiritual development certainly does not preclude such activities). What it means is that they have managed to raise families or have wound down careers or otherwise lost interest in an externally focused life.

The fires of spiritual longing that were kindled in their youth and dwindled as they matured are now flaming up again. But these impulses have shifted, deepened. While their appetite for direct spiritual experience has intensified, they are no longer as motivated by the desire for personal enlightenment (or even the belief in such a thing) as they once were. Their own awakening is intimately entwined with the liberation of all beings. They experience the tribulations of the world in the cells of their own bodies, and they dedicate the fruits of their spiritual efforts to the whole of the human family and to the Earth. They have stepped across the threshold from fertile woman to wise elder, and this new landscape is more wondrous than they could have imagined.

deepening

For this chapter, I'm giving you a freewriting prompt. If you've never done freewriting before, see "Writing Practice Guidelines" on page 223.

Your prompt is this: "My deepest desire is . . ." Let whatever arises in your mind and heart spill onto the page (or screen) as you respond to it. Allow yourself to be surprised—maybe even shocked—by what comes up. Your desires could relate to your sexual appetites or emotional needs. They could be about how you want to embody yourself—or the Divine. Don't hold back. Get naked.

Mother of the World
Tender teacher, fierce friend
Keeper of the jewels

7

SHELTERING

Mothering as a Path of Awakening

opening

This world needs all kinds of women and every kind of mother. Maybe you have not birthed a baby and instead you mother the world. Or your niece and nephew or your friends' kids. Or you adopted a child who came through another woman's body. Or perhaps you have grown a person in your own womb, and the first time you look into the eyes of your baby boy or girl and they look back, you feel your heart is going to explode.

You thought you had loved before—your first boyfriend, for instance, who took his own life at sixteen; your Grandma Rose, who always saw the best and most beautiful in you; your cats; or the father of the new little person you are now holding in your arms. But this is a quantum love leap. It takes your breath away and makes you want to laugh and cry at the same time, and so you are catapulted into hushed astonishment, and there you rest, gazing.

You are paralyzed by joy—yes, of course—and something else. A peripheral pain. You fear that you were destined to mess this thing up, this mothering thing. That no matter how many books you read on conscious child-rearing or how diligently you practice mindfulness, you are bound to get lost in the woods of parenting, dragging your poor kid behind you and doing irreparable damage along the way.

As the years go by, you will not be able to believe the shit that will come out of your mouth sometimes. The very opposite of the ways you are now vowing to speak to your child. You will sound like your shrill Aunt Shirley. There will be times when all you will want is to be left alone, and you will slam your door like a teenager, or grab your keys and drive away, or bellow until your child's eyes grow wide with alarm and you can see the crack forming in their soul like a fault line. You'll know that you put it there.

And as you gaze at your newborn baby now, there is yet a deeper sorrow behind your resignation to failure: you know that you will be unable to protect your beloved child from the pain of this world. You know you will try anyway. Try with all your might. That you will do anything to keep this beloved person from bearing a fraction of the suffering you have endured. That you would die for them.

And you do. To be someone's mother is to die again and again. Die to who you thought you were and who you hoped you would become. Die to your cherished notions of what a child of yours should look like, sound like, behave like. Die to your illusions of control. Control of your own emotions, control of your child's experiences. And in proportion to all your deaths you will be blessed with endless resurrections. You will rise, radiant, from the flames of what you thought was the end of the world. And your child will rise, luminous, from the ashes of your errors.

Then there will be those moments of perfect wholeness—many more of these than the broken ones—when you are driving together to a ballet lesson or the hardware store and a feeling of utter contentment will wash over you. Looking over at the being you call your son or daughter, you will say, "Do you know that you are my favorite person in the world to hang out with?" And they will smile and nod and say, "Me too," meaning this person, your child, wouldn't trade these times with you for anything. And something in your soul will understand that the torn fabric of the world has just been mended a little by the ordinary miracle of your love.

You will not carry responsibility for shepherding this human being through the world by yourself (you cannot). The Great Mother holds you even as you hold your son or daughter. When you feel incapable of making the next decision or even taking the next breath, you will turn to that Mother. You'll lay your head in her lap, unburden your heart, and listen for her guidance. And then, warmed beside her hearth, you will go back into the forest and pick up your baby and continue your journey.

Householder Yoga

Give me a cave in the Himalayas with no heat aside from a smoky fire pit, only the food brought to me by those willing to hike up the mountain, and nothing to do all day but meditate and chant and read the ancient scriptures. Such a sadhana, or spiritual practice, has got to be easier than raising a child, living with her other parent, and trying to make a harmonious home.

What person on a spiritual path who also has a family has not had this thought?

Welcome to Householder Yoga. If *yoga* means "path to union with God," then hooking up with a life partner and having kids together can be as valid—and certainly as rigorous—as living in an ashram engaged in spiritual discipline all day and into the night. And as transformational. Every culture and religious tradition controlled by men has placed higher importance on scriptural study and ritual observance than on feeding babies and cleaning up after them. Women have internalized our own devaluation. No wonder many women with the privilege of making the choice are choosing not to have children. Child-rearing is arguably the most difficult path possible, a hero's journey that leads us on harrowing adventures but for which we receive almost no credit.

So, given that being a parent is such a challenging and unglamorous enterprise, why bother? Because sentient beings are made to. Most of us are, anyway. We're biologically, socially, and spiritually programmed to connect with one another and create new humans. And we are perfectly designed to care for them. The mistakes we make are part of the package. Our fears for their well-being are impossible to circumvent. We are bound to stumble through the experience of being someone's mom, just as our mothers fumbled through their own motherly missions. Maybe with more awareness than they did, but not with any more certainty.

My own kid karma has been endlessly bewildering to me. I adopted two children of mixed race who had been abused in their families of origin. I fell so deeply in love with them I couldn't imagine adoring a child conceived and ripened in my own uterus any more fully. One of these daughters moved far away, both geographically and emotionally, though she will always be my first child and holds a singular seat on a lotus in my heart. The other one died. My two older stepdaughters have always been kind, but a bit reserved. They don't climb into bed with me and cry when they're sad, and I'm not the first (or even the fifth) person they text with good news. I have wistfully commented to their dad that I think they see me as a secretary from Iowa—harmless, but a little boring (with no offense to actual secretaries from Iowa).

My youngest stepdaughter, Kali, is different. She is as much my child as my own children have ever been. My youngest, Jenny, and I moved in with Ganga Das and Kali when our girls were both nine, and we became the family I had longed to give birth to. Those were the sweetest years of my life. I gave myself over to mothering Jenny and Kali. Science projects and first periods, birthday parties and unrequited crushes. The two girls were inseparable, and the relationship between them brought me great joy.

After Jenny's sudden death at fourteen, Kali went to stay with her mom and never came back. I lost my family overnight. At first I could not understand why Kali would withdraw from me, both physically and emotionally, at a time when I felt we urgently needed the refuge of each other. We were the two people who loved Jenny most and whom she had most deeply loved. But Jenny's death plunged Kali into turmoil and confusion, and it took years for her to integrate the trauma of losing her beloved sister and best friend and to sort out who I was to her now that Jenny was gone.

Little by little, as she entered young adulthood, Kali made her way back into my life and began to rest again in the safety of my love. There was something in me, though, that held myself back. Not wanting to squash the fragile flower of our reconnection with smothering mothering nor trespass on her loyalty to her own mom, I maintained a tender yet spacious footing with my stepdaughter.

Until one day around ten years after Jenny's death when Ganga Das and I were traveling in France. Our friend Andrew had offered his tiny apartment in Chartres for a few days so that we could explore the cathedral, famous for its iconic labyrinth, its elaborate rose windows, and most of all for its Black Madonna—a statue of the Blessed Mother that exudes a quality of the primordial feminine, a being who both encompasses and transcends the Virgin Mary.

That day, as Ganga Das and I walked around the cathedral in the rain, talking about our children, I felt a rush of pain about the distance between Kali and me, and I started to cry. I admitted that I was tired of holding myself back for fear of violating her boundaries. I was ready to let go. I wanted to help Kali with her graduate school applications and listen to her concerns about current events, buy her things I saw that I knew she would love and take her with me to some of the amazing places where I was invited to teach, without fear of transgression.

"Well, then go ahead and mother her," a voice resounded in my mind. "What have you been waiting for?" In that moment, a stone lifted from my heart. I realized that I didn't need to wait for Kali's approval of my plan. Nor did I require that she reciprocate my dedication to her. I could simply unlock the gates and get on with loving her as my daughter. This did not negate her relationship with her mother. It simply affirmed what was true for me.

I did not rush home and tell Kali about my epiphany. I just quietly acted on it. I reclaimed our bond and treated her as my own child, an adult child now, but still young and vulnerable. Kali was strong and passionate about human rights and climate change and spiritual awakening—the very same issues I was passionate about! Without my saying a word, Kali began to respond to my maternal devotion. She started coming by for tea. We'd talk about her plans for founding a nonprofit to make art with underserved children, or she'd fill me in on her love life. We'd reminisce about Jenny, sometimes with tears, but more often laughing over Jenny's adorable idiosyncrasies, which the two of us can recall more vividly than anyone else ever could. Kali and I have grown closer since the Holy Mother came to me outside her home in Chartres, woke me up, and reopened my own Mother Heart.

MY MOM

I have a mother who has transformed over the course of her lifetime from a free spirit into a wise elder, and along the way she taught me what it is to be a woman. A bereaved mother herself, she lost our older brother, Matty, to a brain tumor when he was ten, and for a time we lost her to the wilderness of grief. But over the years, my mom integrated this harrowing experience and picked the mantle of motherhood back up. She has modeled for me what it looks like to shatter and mend, to defy social norms and find your own voice, to place beauty over safety and generosity over profit. Susanna's vulnerability has given me permission to be vulnerable, and her ferocity has allowed me to be fierce. Her overflowing love of life has shown me what true happiness looks like.

My mom never shows up at our house without bearing bags or boxes or baskets of treasures she picked up at yard sales or at the local thrift store. Incomplete sets of hand-blown Mexican water glasses carefully wrapped ("Who needs exactly eight?"). An alpaca sweater, extra small ("Perfect for you"). A challah ("To stash in the freezer for french toast") or chocolate chip cookies from a bake sale ("For when the kids come over," she says 100 percent of the time, referring to her great-grandchildren, who occasionally stop by). She reads what I write, even when it is excessively theistic (while she tends toward pantheism) and unfailingly pronounces it profound and moving. I can spin out and lose my shit with her, enumerating my collection of stressors in a shrill voice, and she will calmly bear witness, identify just enough with my victim trip to make me feel supported, and then suggest a variety of practical solutions, most of which are right on target. She doesn't complain about her health or her partner or her business. Our time together is almost always about me.

I cannot imagine stepping up to the call that's been seeping through the seams of my life if I didn't have this calm, complicated, unconditionally loving being holding my hand.

ASHA

Taking on family life as an opportunity for spiritual transformation requires vigilance, humility, and the ability to see the cosmic joke in the midst of our children's fractured digits and our partner's flirtations with people who aren't us. Praising God by praising our kindergartener's first painting. Worshiping at the altar of the kitchen stove, making offerings of rice and veggies and blueberry muffins to the Holy One. Bowing to the Beloved in the form of an angry teenager or a needy spouse. And most of all welcoming the presence of the sacred in every cell of our body while singing our daughter to sleep, or watching her eyelids flutter in the mornings when we wake her for school, or catching our partner gazing at us in adoration as we cuddle our little ones close, explaining why the baby bird that fell out of the nest will never fly.

Asha Greer is a lifelong friend and mentor. A visionary artist and Sufi teacher, Asha is the cofounder of Lama, the interspiritual community in the mountains of northern New Mexico where I grew up. As the mother of four girls, Asha recognized early on that unless she focused on parenting as a spiritual practice, she would have no spiritual life. When I left home at fourteen and moved to Lama Foundation, Asha was my "guardian." This made it possible for a minor like me to live there on my own. She didn't try to parent me, but she did pay attention to my physical well-being and spiritual development.

Asha's complicated marriage to a charismatic spiritual leader came to a dramatic end in the midst of community life. It was also community that saved her. The people she lived with at Lama flowed into the spaces left behind when Asha was falling apart, granting her the capacity to be more present for her children the rest of the time.

Six feet tall and sturdy as a great tree, Asha is on the opposite end of the physical spectrum from me (I'm less than five feet tall and not much over a hundred pounds). Her personality is direct to the point of being brusque, and her mind is brilliantly original, so that the most startling things come spontaneously tumbling from her mouth. She makes little distinction between famous spiritual luminaries and children, offering each being her disarming attention and freely dispensing her unorthodox wisdom. Asha is one of the most present people on the planet.

"Family is the most powerful spiritual teacher I have ever known," Asha told me (and she has known many teachers, all of whom at one time or another passed through Lama). "It pokes you and wakes you up. It's easy to become complacent on the spiritual path, to start thinking you know something and have freed yourself from your bad habits. No matter where you are in your practice, family can undercut your awakened state and pull you right out of the present moment." She acknowledged that when you have young children it's almost impossible to maintain a spiritual practice ("or an artistic practice," Asha added, which for her is the same thing). Your family has to *be* your practice. And the opportunities for practicing are abundant!

"Don't be fooled," Asha reminded me. "Most of the spiritual books that have influenced us were written by men in societies where women were not included. You've been programmed by a lot of dead men who had no idea what it is to be a woman." Women are learning to resacralize our ordinary embodied experience. We are no longer willing to wait for invitations from men's ancient elite clubs; we do not believe true spiritual experience is limited to these privileged spaces. Instead, we find the face of the Holy One in the faces of our babies and our lovers, our elders and our coworkers, the dirty dishes and the deep quiet that falls over our homes when everyone else is sleeping and we stand at the window, looking at the moon.

God-the-Mother

For the Christian mystic Julian of Norwich, it was obvious that God is a mother.

That wasn't Julian's real name, by the way. The woman we know as Julian of Norwich was an anonymous medieval anchoress who walled herself into a small cell attached to the St. Julian's Church in Norwich, England, where she produced some of the most stunning and subversive writings in the history of Christendom. While the majority of her time was spent in prayer and contemplation, Julian also cultivated a garden in a small courtyard adjoining her anchorage, and she kept bees. She was not a hermit, however. The anchoress kept designated hours at a window that opened onto the busy streets of Norwich, from which she offered counsel to the townspeople about everything from the deaths of their loved ones to the interpretation of their dreams.

The most controversial of Julian's teachings was her declaration of God-the-Mother. The second person of the Trinity, Julian reasoned, had to be female, because who but a mother would break herself open and pour herself out for love of her children? This is what Christ did, Julian reminds us. He incarnated for love. And this is what he continues to do. Like a loving mother, Christ takes a personal interest in every single being, forgiving us when we screw up and rejoicing when we return to love. "Only He who is our true Mother and source of all life may rightfully be called by this name," Julian wrote, sweeping aside gender binaries. "Nature, love, wisdom and knowledge are all attributes of the Mother, which is God."

How did she get away with this? you might ask. Was the patriarchy on vacation when Julian proclaimed the Motherhood of the Divine? Were men more tolerant in the Middle Ages? Hardly! Julian hid her writings under her bed. And after she died, a protégé (also anonymous) spirited the pages away, where they were more or less lost in obscurity for about five hundred years before being rediscovered and translated from Middle English to modern English at the turn of the twentieth century. Julian, a contemporary of Chaucer, was the first woman to write in English. Because she was not permitted to learn Latin, the language of the church, the only way for her to express herself was in the vernacular.

It's not as if Julian suddenly decided to risk everything and speak out about God. A near-death experience impelled her. When Julian was thirty, having borne witness to three rounds of the plague—estimated to have wiped out a third of the population of England (which means at least three out of every ten people Julian knew and loved died a terrible death)—she became gravely ill herself. Her mother called the priest to administer last rites. The cleric held a crucifix above Julian's face, instructing her to gaze at the suffering Christ on the cross, assuring her that when she died she would go directly to heaven to be with him.

As Julian stared at her crucified Beloved, the room around her began to fade, and Jesus sprang to life. In a series of visions she calls "The Showings," Christ revealed to Julian the nature of the Universe (Love) and of the human soul (Love) and of God's attitude toward all of creation (unmitigated, unconditional Love). When, against all odds, she recovered her health, how could she do anything else but write it all down so that she would never forget it? Julian insists that she wasn't trying to correct the "Holy Mother Church" in reporting the details of the teachings she received. She was simply testifying as accurately as she could to the blessing of her own experience.

It was clear to Julian that Christ made these revelations, not for her alone, but for all humanity. So she pledged her life to God and to living what he (she) had revealed. She entered the anchorage and contemplated the notes she had initially made of everything Christ said to her (known as the "short text"). Then, over the course of twenty years, Julian proceeded to write commentaries on each the sixteen showings (known as the "long text"). I had the great fortune of translating this masterpiece into contemporary English.

Julian of Norwich understood that the Divine Essence embodies the full range of feminine qualities, from mercy in response to wickedness to courage in the face of danger, from "homey friendliness" to passion. God-the-Mother encourages us in states of paralyzing doubt, even as she challenges us to subvert entrenched systems of power and authority and cultivate a direct relationship with the Holy in the temple (or anchorage!) of our own souls.

Loving Each Other

On the spiritual path, the Beloved asks only two things of us: that we love him and that we love each other. This is all we have to strive for. . . . In my opinion, the most reliable sign that we are following both these teachings is that we are loving each other. . . . Be assured that the more progress you make in loving your neighbor, the greater will be your love for God. His Majesty loves us so much that he repays us for loving our neighbor by increasing our love for him in a thousand ways. I cannot doubt this. . . . Oh, friends! I can clearly see how important love of your neighbor is to some of you, and how others of you just don't seem to care. If only you could understand how vital this virtue is to all of us, you wouldn't engage in any other study. TERESA OF ÁVILA

Wherever we hover on the gender spectrum, if we identify as female at all, the company of other women can be singularly healing. Mothers and daughters making a meal together or figuring out a profit-and-loss statement; one sister consoling another in the wake of a romantic betrayal; introverted friends hoisting themselves out of the safe cave of their homes for a birthday celebration and lifting their glasses to praise the birthday girl, one by one, in detail.

Women singing together, in unison or harmony, softly crooning to the dying or belting out the blues. Women gathering for ceremony: honoring the harvest moon or the spring equinox, the birth of someone's first grandchild or the onset of menstruation. Women getting together to write letters of protest to their state representatives or peacefully demonstrating in the streets, willingly getting arrested. Women teaching each other how to meditate, or play the flute, or speak Spanish, or sharing enough of a working knowledge of the carbon cycle to be able to meaningfully engage in climate activism. Women holding onto each other as we navigate the criminal justice system or embedded discrimination in the workplace. Women being willing to engage in difficult conversations with each other about white privilege and systemic racism. Women organizing formal gatherings for a common cause or informal clusterings just for fun.

Women soothe each other's nervous systems, make it safe to open our hearts, create a listening vessel for our pain and a cheering squad for our accomplishments. (And sometimes we call each other on our shit, which we endeavor to do with tenderness and courage, humor and humility.)

Female relationships take manifold forms. Some women do not have a mom to remind them of who they really are (a radiant being worthy of everything good). So we can adopt one. There are lonesome mothers everywhere in need of a daughter to adore. They exist in kindly neighbors and invisible authors, in Mata Durga and Mother Mary and Mother Earth.

Some moms are no longer alive, and we ache for their embrace; we can be still, close our eyes, and tune in to that part of ourselves and that part of her that are always and forever united. We can talk to her while we drive home from the grocery store or plant lettuce. We can call on the spirits of our ancestors—our Polish grandmothers and our Lebanese great-grandmothers and our African great-great-grandmothers—for guidance and confidence and a better sense of humor.

Those of us who have not had children can harness all that unspent maternal energy and go forth and mother the world or pick someone especially in need of our motherly love and mother them.

Those of us without sisters can make our friends into our sisters or borrow someone else's. Our students can be our daughters, and our teachers can be our aunties. When we do not have a close female friend, we can light a candle and sit on our knees and ask the Divine Mother to send us one. Or we can find her in the pages of good literature, in the notes of every kind of music, among peace activists and spiritual guides. They do not have to even know we exist for us to draw sustenance from our relationship with them. But we have to leave the door of our hearts open so that they can slip in.

Some of us have been so deeply damaged by our mothers that we recoil from the company of women. The whole notion of a Divine Mother may trigger our woundedness around the ways we were or weren't mothered. There is no reason to force a connection to the sacred feminine. Maybe our true home rests in formlessness. We may find refuge in the holy emptiness, devoid of binary characteristics, free from traumatic associations. The more we seek and attend to what is real inside the holy temple of our own hearts, the more we will find healthy and loving manifestations of her in the world.

When our connection with the women in our lives has been strained or severed, we can either let these women go with love or fight with all our might to get them back. For some, the Divine Mother, in the form of Kali or Durga, Mary or Gaia, becomes a vital and living being who heals our ruptured relationship with our moms, sisters, friends.

None of these beloved women may look anything like our preconceived notions of mother, sister, daughter, friend, mentor. But our hearts will recognize her. We can post a lookout in our hearts, cast a message in a bottle on the ocean of our longing. We can risk letting women matter to us.

Mothering the World

Many of the women in my life do not have children, either because of infertility, or because they never hooked up with the "right" partner, or because they consciously chose not to procreate. And every one of these women is in some way mothering the world.

My friend Saraswati has surrendered to not birthing a child. It just didn't work out. She tried with her first husband and tried with her second, both of whom came to the relationship with children of their own. Saraswati is a doctor of oriental medicine who specializes in women's health. The vulnerability that accompanies her own fertility issues make her even more available to her patients; she is determined to help them get to the bottom of their concerns and also sympathetic and supportive when there is no solution.

Saraswati is also a yoga teacher. I have watched her pour her motherly energy onto her students, and I see how they soften and unfold in her presence. I myself have been one of those thirsty saplings that green up when I practice with Saraswati. Choosing to focus her beam on women has created a safe and vibrant space for the feminine to flourish.

In yoga literature, Saraswati tells me, we discover that the word *hatha* (asana practice) contains the roots of the words for sun (*ha*) and moon (*tha*). The solar element is about constancy;

when you look at the sun, it's always the same—a disk of fiery light that sets at the end of each day and rises again the next morning. The moon appears to be different every day as she cycles through her phases. She is in flux. She darkens and hides. She blooms and shines.

"Hatha yoga is the study of opposites," Saraswati says. "It's not about polarity, but about connecting and relating." The masculine aspect of our being learns to cultivate softness, and the feminine learns to cultivate stillness. Just as the fluctuating mind reflects a lack of equilibrium, so are our beings out of balance when we deny the value of the emotional, the dark, the hidden. "It's time to reclaim the power of sensitivity, empathy, the capacity to be with," Saraswati says. In other words, it's time to reclaim the feminine.

Brady is another woman who skipped householder yoga and has dedicated her life to the dharma (Buddhist spiritual teachings). It was one of those choiceless choices. Brady was open to marriage and family. "I always thought I'd have six children," Brady told me. "Later . . . later . . . and then it got to be later." No husband; no kids. Instead, Brady has spent more than twenty years immersed in Tibetan Buddhism. She lived in a monastery in Nepal for five of those years. And for an entire year she lived in a box.

The floor of this traditional monastic practice space was around three feet by three feet. The box was open at the top, with a shelf in front on which to read sacred texts and a space underneath to store them. It was too small to lie down in—an intentional feature meant to prevent the practitioner from going fully unconscious, so that part of them stays present even in sleep—and Brady slept sitting up. Her constant companion was the sciatica with which she entered and which grew more intense as the year unfolded. This spinal pain helped connect Brady with the suffering of the world, deepening her compassion and strengthening her aspiration to help all sentient beings become free.

There are many ways to show up in the feminine. Some expressions of the feminine are gentle, soft, classically nurturing. In other women it carries the swordlike quality to cut through illusion and enable them to speak truth to power. For some of us, another human being is a portal to the Divine. Others cultivate a direct connection with the Beloved in the chamber of their own hearts and also out in the world, finding traces of the Holy One in everyone.

Women, whether in our biology, our identities, our spiritual practice, or our work, hear the cries of the world resounding in the ganglia of our own nervous systems. The milk of our soul comes rushing forth to feed the hungry and comfort the frightened.

ANIMAL FAMILY

In my family of origin, one of my nicknames was "Saint Francis." As a small child on Long Island, I was preternaturally patient about connecting with animals, both wild and domestic (a skill that never did extend to my human relations). I begged my folks for a pet of my own. Reluctant to take on a dog or cat, my parents agreed to a bird. We adopted Enrique, a yellow canary, when I was nine. His cage hung in the kitchen, and it was understood that it would be my job to make sure he had fresh water, feed him the right amount of birdseed, and replace his newspaper floor every few days. I took my canary responsibilities seriously (as I took just about every matter throughout my childhood).

But I also reveled in my bird's companionship. I taught Enrique to sing. I mean, of course he already knew how to sing—he was a canary—but I made up elaborate whistling games, starting with simple three-note melodies and gradually expanding to more complex musical patterns. Enrique learned them all, cocking his head and watching my mouth with his tiny black eyes and then repeating everything I sang to him, including subtle rhythmic variations. Enrique seemed to be pleased with himself after each of these jam sessions. He would fluff up his downy breast and give himself a satisfying shake. It felt like a canary high five.

One evening, after coming home from a movie (I remember exactly what it was: *Little Big Man*, with Dustin Hoffman), we found Enrique upside-down on the floor of his cage, dead. I could not figure out what I had done wrong, though I mentally combed through any possible indicators I might have missed that Enrique was unwell. I think it was my dad who finally figured it out. We had recently had our pantry repainted, located only a few feet from Enrique's cage. The fumes must have asphyxiated him. I was sure that it was really because I had gone out for the evening and Enrique missed me so much he died of a broken heart.

Over the years, although my desire to adopt every stray of every species has only slightly subsided, I found ways to love animals without bringing them all home with me. I have stood very still for deer and mountain goats, willing them to accept my presence. I greet the ravens in the trees surrounding our house, certain that they know me. I stop to pet every dog I encounter out for a walk on city streets or hiking in the wilderness. And I have also had dogs of my own whom I have loved beyond all reason and who loved me with equal devotion. Each one has lifted and carried me through some of life's most grueling moments, allowing me to discharge my unspent maternal energy into their endlessly receptive dog hearts.

I am not alone in my passion for animals. Many of my friends and acquaintances, especially single people and childless couples, treat their animals as family. Not only is it valid for our pets to occupy a place of primary emotional connection in our lives, but I believe the love we share with these nonhuman beings contributes to uplifting the heart of the world.

deepening

Write a letter to a child as if you knew you were going to die soon, passing along what you most wish for them to know. What is your deepest wisdom, your highest truth? The things that delight you, in which you'd like the child also to take delight? Secrets you are ready to reveal or heroes who have inspired you? Distill the essence of your legacy. (For help with this writing, see "Writing Practice Guidelines" on page 223.)

The skies are broken
Mother Earth cries out in pain
The web of life mends

▼▼▼▼▼▼▼▼▼▼▼▼▼▼▼▼▼

8

COCREATING

Caring for Our Mother the Earth

opening

She is your Mother. Maybe you're the sibling who never left home. Well, not for long, anyway. Perhaps you are one of those kids who heads off to seek your fortune, lasts about five minutes out on the dirty city streets, and then moves back in with your mom. And she's one of those mothers that nods supportively when her offspring claim we are ready to make it on our own, and then when we drag our dispirited asses back home, she welcomes us with strawberry rhubarb pie.

She is your Mother the Earth, and you belong to her. She nurtured you in her dark belly, birthed you in joy, and sustains you at great cost to herself. You have slept in her forests, beneath the safety of her canopy. You have cupped her snowmelt in your hands. You have investigated the life hidden beneath the surface of her deserts, skied her alpine slopes, and biked her slickrock canyons. You have reveled in her generosity and been grateful.

She has never asked much of you in return. Up until now, your gratitude has been enough. Your delight has been her reward. Up until now, she has not needed you as you have needed her. But that is shifting. You have grown up, and your Mother the Earth is in peril. She cannot hide her distress from you, and you would not want her to. You are mature enough to handle the truth.

"Tell me what is troubling you, Mama," you whisper, exactly as she always spoke to you when you were small and frightened and bleeding from some injury (real or imagined).

"Pretty much everything, honey," she answers. Her smile is rueful.

She sits up against the sky, the clouds of her hair in beauteous disarray. The mountains of her breasts still tumble luxuriously, and the ample valley of her lap is as accommodating as ever. Her cloak is showing signs of wear: the fabric of trees is threadbare where old growth forests have been clear-cut, and the woodlands that remain are on fire. Her hot flashes that began years ago have not abated, though she has tried every concoction of herbs; in fact, they are growing more intense, making it difficult to sleep at night. The rivers and creeks and waterfalls of her bloodstream flow more sluggishly, brackish and fetid in places where they used to be limpid.

"I'll get through this," she says. "You're not getting rid of your old Ma so easily." She reaches down to smooth the crease between your brows. "It's you kids I'm worried about."

It's not you in particular. It's your wayward siblings and their guileless offspring. Some of your brothers couldn't get away fast enough from your Mother the Earth. They made their home on the moonscape of urban America, ran for public office and forgot why, got drunk on power and privilege and struck backroom deals that squandered your inheritance while their Mother the Earth still breathed and ached and shook her head in bewilderment.

You have tried to intervene, but your prodigal siblings won't speak to you. The boys, mostly. The girls who align with their brothers against your mother have become boys themselves, for all practical purposes. They have abdicated their sensuality, forsaken their vulnerability, learned to play the boys' games, and learned to play them well. They have convinced themselves that they do not need their Mother the Earth.

But when they cannot breathe and they have nothing to eat, they will stagger their way home to her, and she will welcome them with a feast in their honor. You will help her in the kitchen, humming as you chop the onions and stir the stew.

Incarnational

Instead of engaging spiritual practice as a contraption to catapult us up and out of this relative world, the feminine mystic shows up right here, in the center of the incarnational experience. We bless the messy wonder of it all, the experience of being human.

This is where we encounter the face of the Holy One. We are not infatuated with transcendence; what we want is authenticity. We're not worried about the senses, with their appetites and inconsistencies; to us the body is sacred. We're not striving to reach the Pure Land of desirelessness. This makes no sense to the feminine, for whom desire is neither evil nor unspiritual, for whom pleasure can be another form of prayer. The sacred shines from the naked heart of what *is*, in this manifest miracle, in this very shape.

The solutions to the environmental crises that threaten to eradicate life lie in the feminine response. Rather than delineate perpetrators and victims, sacred and profane, physical and metaphysical, the feminine welcomes everyone to the table. Like the Great Mother herself, the feminine mystic does not view creation as a damaged object in need of repair but rather as a beloved child in need of care.

Effective activism arises from unconditional love.

Mending the World

There is a kabbalistic story in which the boundless, formless, unified Holy One wished to know its Holy Self, and so it contracted and poured itself into vessels. But the Divine Radiance was too much for these limited containers, and so they shattered, scattering shards of broken light across the universe, giving birth to all that is.

This sounds like modern cosmology, which also asserts that the universe expanded from an exceedingly high-density state, resulting in the full spectrum of material phenomena. I've dubbed this vessel-shattering version of the origins of the universe "the Jewish big bang." It comes from a teaching Rabbi Isaac Luria offered in the sixteenth century to illustrate how form arises from formlessness, how light gets trapped inside darkness, and how the Holy One needs us to participate in the unfolding goodness of creation. Humans, as the teaching goes, were created to excavate and lift the shards of light from the dense predicament of existence and restore the vessels to wholeness.

In mystical Judaism, this teaching is known as *tikkun olam*, the mending of the world. How are we to do this? The answer is: with every act of chesed (loving-kindness) and *tzedakah* (generosity). It means observing the directives found in the Torah (which we can view not only as the compendium of Hebrew scriptures but as the essence of all the sacred teachings of all the world's great wisdom traditions). It means cultivating a contemplative practice to nurture intimacy with the Divine, making an effort to welcome the stranger and care for the Earth. It means bending close to listen for what it is our sisters and brothers on the margins might need (and being willing to forgo our notions of what "helping" looks like, since our preconceived ideas of service sometimes get in the way of authentically serving). It means pressing our ear to the land to hear the heartbeat of the Mother, learning to read her pulses, diagnose her ailments, intuit healing remedies. It means slowing down enough to let the pain of the world all the way into our hearts, allowing our hearts to break open, and acting from that broken-open space. It means stepping up with humility, with curiosity, with love.

EMBRACING THE FEMININE IN ACTIVISM

Our global climate crisis demands that we break our habits of overconsumption and engage in voluntary simplicity. This is the antithesis of the dominant culture's emphasis on power through acquisition and the primacy of the individual. Yet it is the quintessence of the feminine values of cooperation and generosity. The masculine paradigm is predicated on scarcity, while the feminine is rooted in abundance for all. When I speak of masculine and feminine values I do not mean the literal male and female. I am not blaming environmental degradation and economic injustice exclusively on men and suggesting that women are neither materialistic nor greedy. I am invoking deeper, indwelling qualities reflected in conventional gender disparities and showing up in both women and men (and in girls and boys). Because both religion and politics, historically intermeshed, have been dominated by systems that empower men and oppress women, essential feminine values have been subverted, and this imbalance is reflected in the way we treat nature and one another.

If encountering this challenge to meet the needs of the environment elicits a vaguely guilty feeling in you, accompanied by a white-knuckled intention to tighten your belt, I invite you to relax. That's the shadow of the masculine paradigm designed to blame you for not being perfect. The feminine is not about some preconception of purity, which we could never hope to attain and which is therefore destined for failure. The way of the feminine mystic is to adore the presence of the sacred in all things. It's about celebrating life—food, sex, beauty—not denying life.

So how do we claim this life-affirming birthright without sucking our Mother the Earth dry? By engaging the very feminine values that have been missing from our religious and political institutions: the willingness to be present, to listen, and, most of all, to allow our hearts to be moved by the suffering of the world. The great gift of the brokenhearted is a deepening of care. When we have fully faced the injustices that rage like wildfires on the margins of society and across the wildernesses of the planet, we cannot help but offer ourselves in service. We bleed for our bleeding Mother. We spontaneously rise to tend her.

HEALING VESSELS

While the cosmological story of mending the shattered vessels of the universe serves as a parable for compassionate action, my friend Cynthia Jurs is literally offering vessels filled with healing prayers to the Earth. She calls this practice the Earth Treasure Vase Global Healing Project. Almost thirty years ago, when Cynthia—a practitioner of Tibetan Buddhism—was in Nepal, she climbed high up into the Himalayas to meet a 106-year-old lama who lived as a hermit in a cave at more than

13,000 feet of elevation. "What can I do to bring healing and protection to the Earth?" was the way Cynthia finally formed the amorphous question burning in her being as she walked.

Heartbroken by the looming climate crisis, Cynthia, like most of us, would have done anything to tend the wounds of the Mother. The Rinpoche (a recognized reincarnation of a very high religious leader) shared an ancient practice that involved offering prayers and intentions while filling a clay vessel with sacred objects and then burying it in a region in need of healing. With the Rinpoche's support and connections, Cynthia and her sangha, her spiritual community, commissioned the creation of thirty earthenware vases and had them hand delivered the following spring to Cynthia's home in Santa Fe, New Mexico, by friends who had been visiting Nepal.

Since then, the treasure vases have been buried in conflict zones and areas of environmental devastation all over the world—from Liberia to South Africa, from the Amazon jungle to the American Southwest, from New Guinea to New York—creating a global mandala of restorative prayer. Cynthia shared with me that only after carrying many of these vases around the planet did it dawn on her that this practice of bringing protection to the Earth was addressing her own need for healing as well. Having been abused as a girl, with the associated loss of her family's support, Cynthia quietly carried her own brokenness into her spiritual quest. Although she clearly perceived that the ways in which women are abused is reflected in the ways we exploit the Earth, Cynthia was less connected to her own story of violation and disenfranchisement. Her recognition of her own vulnerability has deepened—and more deeply integrated—an already profound practice, grounding her Earth activism in the full reality of the human experience.

At first, as she fully faced the suffering of the Earth, Cynthia's heartbreak felt like almost too much to bear. The wreckage, after all, seems unending. Toxic waste is dumped into the watershed. Young girls are abducted and sold as sex slaves. Multinational banks are getting bigger at the expense of those who have nothing. Meanwhile, Cynthia's personal losses compounded. When she discovered that one of her most beloved teachers had a history of using his position to procure and abuse fifteen-year-old girls—the same age Cynthia was when she was raped—she severed her connection with him. Now not only had she lost most of her family of origin but she had lost her primary spiritual family, too. Unfettered by lineage, Cynthia was launched into the unknown with nothing but her treasure-vase practice and her longing to be of some use in this precious, fractured realm. The Earth herself became Cynthia's source of authority—both the teacher and the teaching (the Buddha and the dharma).

As it turns out, the Great Mother has a lot to say. "The earth is not just calling, she's screaming," Cynthia told me. "The treasure-vase practice is changing from something we are doing to something we are being. We must all become the vessels for healing in this world." Cynthia emphasizes that one of the most important elements in this process is dropping our preconceived notions of what healing is supposed to look like. "The conceptual mind can't figure it out," she says. "The need is too great. It's overwhelming."

And so we let our hearts guide us. We let our bodies guide us. "When we align ourselves with our deepest prayer, the next right thing unfolds," Cynthia discovered. This is the way of the feminine mystic. We cannot be expected to be sanctioned by the hierarchical structures that have let us down and left us out. But neither should we reject them. Each tradition carries wisdom jewels we can gather and plant in the earth.

Some Buddhist practitioners, like Cynthia, believe that as the teachings of the Buddha ripen in the garden of community, they become more universal. Cynthia is excited to see the dharma unfolding toward a collective awakening.

This shared task of awakening is infused with the Sacred Feminine, grounded in the knowing that we belong to the web of interbeing and that it is only by surrendering to this belonging that we can hope to mend the world.

Stewardship

Sometimes it's embarrassing to be an American. The United States is among a handful of countries to pull its support out from under the already flimsy Paris climate accord. But the government and the people are two different entities. Inspired by the feminine ideals of community and hospitality, increasingly larger circles of us are coming together to develop solutions to the imminent threat of global extinction. We are scoping out ways to jump off the train of overconsumption and simplify our lives. We are growing food in small gardens and sharing the bounty with our hungry neighbors. We are buying and trading and making what we need and learning to say, "No, thank you" to the endless stuff society tries to tell us we have to have but which we could easily live without—and finding the deeper satisfaction in doing so.

One of the most comprehensive documents I know of that promotes sustainability is the Earth Charter, drafted at the turn of this new millennium, in 1999. Like the Universal Declaration of Human Rights, which was developed in the wake of the Nazi Holocaust of the mid-twentieth century, the Earth Charter is considered to be a "soft legal document"—morally, if not legally, binding to governments that embrace the core tenets. A collaboration of many different nations, the Earth Charter was born as a United Nations initiative and brought to fruition by civil society.

The Earth Charter is an inclusive response to the climate catastrophe and associated social justice issues. Its core principles include respect and care for the community of life; ecological integrity; social and economic justice; and democracy, nonviolence, and peace. It invites us to imagine a new way of living together, in harmony with the planet we share. This global agreement is grounded in the recognition of what the Holy Feminine has always known: we are all interrelated and interdependent. We are children in the midst of a perilous adventure, and we are responsible for one another. Both unity and diversity are equally sacred realities. Finding our rightful place in this glorious web of mutuality is a cause for celebration.

A few years ago I was invited to accompany a team from the Global Peace Initiative of Women to a conference in Costa Rica called "The Inner Dimensions of Climate Change." The gathering was convened to help encourage youth activists struggling on the front lines of Earth activism. Mature climate scientists, environmental professionals, and spiritual teachers served as mentors for youth activists from all over Latin America and the Caribbean. "Mentoring" largely consisted of cultivating a stance of loving listening rather than imposing our own notions of what these superheroes should be doing differently.

Most of the young people were indigenous, and many were in danger for their lives as a result of speaking out against colonialism and the industrialization of their natural and cultural heritage. From Honduras to Venezuela, these youths had witnessed the disappearance of loved ones who dared to challenge the imperialist agenda of multinational corporations, and almost all of them knew of someone who had been found dead after attempting to organize their communities to keep their sacred lands unspoiled.

We met in a remote jungle lodge for five days of conversation and meditation, sharing meals and music and laughter, sitting together in a safe and sacred space that allowed these brave beings to tell stories and share ideas, to celebrate and grieve. My task was to lead a circle of lament, in which each young person had the opportunity to express both her pain and her hope. It is one of the great honors and inspirations of my life to have been able to bear witness to the broken hearts of beings so close to the core of the Earth's distress as they took refuge in a circle of loving elders and allowed themselves to fully feel their pain.

What I came away with is this: in spite of the mounting evidence to the contrary, there is ample cause to be optimistic about the future. Despair comes easy when we set up a duality in which human beings are reduced to the categories of perpetrator or victim, the ones who make a mess and those of us who have to clean it up, those who care and the "others" who never will. Hope is kindled when we remember that we belong to one another. By dropping our impulse to otherize, reclaiming our kinship with all life, and embracing the Earth as our Mother, we can collectively awaken from this dangerous dream of dominance and take up the privilege of stewardship that all the great wisdom traditions remind us is our true task.

GAIA

In Greek mythology, the primal energy of the universe is embodied in the Earth goddess Gaia. Wide-Breasted Gaia created herself from the goddess Chaos, and all that we know came into being with her. Deeply rooted in the land itself, Gaia embraces and nourishes all life. Everything arises from her and returns to her. Gaia is more a power than an entity. She is life itself. She is Mother Earth.

In the 1970s a group of scientists developed the Gaia theory, which proposes that the earth is a single organism and that all life is interdependent, forming a synergistic system. This living being is self-regulating and is always seeking balance. The Gaia hypothesis allows us to visualize ourselves as an integral part of the whole and can impel us to stay connected with nature and do everything in our power to tend to and heal her.

Gaia, the mythic goddess, spontaneously came into being, without being created by some external force or driven by some utilitarian agenda. This is the feminine principle. She is being for the sake of being, beauty for the sake of beauty. We are entwined with the Earth. We belong to her, and we *are* her. If the Earth is sacred, then so are we. The material of our existence is fundamentally blessed.

HOLY WATERS

The feminine gets that stewardship of the Earth is not merely a matter of developing technological solutions. It is about deep attentiveness to the Earth herself. Attention with love. My friend Pat McCabe is a spiritual leader from the Diné (Navajo) Nation, where she is also known as Woman Stands Shining. Aptly named, Pat is rising up and radiating, unapologetically speaking on behalf of the Mother. Her advocacy begins with relationship. She listens to the fractured land, talks to the broken water, communicates with the aching air.

One morning a few years ago, Pat awoke to a flood in her high desert yard. The water was rapidly rising and heading for the house. Anticipating the damage and associated costs she could not afford, Pat started to panic. She tried ignoring it, hoping that it would go away, but it only grew bigger. Finally, she recognized what was happening as a sacred event. She decided to engage the water in dialogue. First, she formally introduced herself, and then she welcomed the water. "What do you need, sister?" she asked. "Do you have something to say to my community?"

The moment Pat showed up in this way, she became aware that the spirits were speaking to her. They told her that her people were getting very good at praying but that this was not enough. Now we had to make ourselves available for the answers. This meant opening space for the unexpected and potentially accommodating dramatic change. It could involve what looked at first like loss, for the solutions our souls are crying out for are drastic ones. But we had to be brave and humble enough to allow the truth to reveal itself.

The spirits let Pat know that welcoming the water was a step in the direction of right relationship and that her task was to teach the world about cultivating dialogue with all of life. This, Pat understood, is the feminine way. It is about embracing spirit in form. Here is where the holy dwells: in the cells of our own bodies, in the veins of water that course below the surface of the earth, in the clouds that lift and carry our prayers, mingle them with the prayers of our ancestors, and release them where they are most needed.

After Pat's conversation with water, she had to go out of town to give a lecture in a distant city. When she returned home, the water had divided into two streams, bypassing her house altogether. Not an iota of damage had been done to Pat's home. "This was her solution," Pat says, clearly impressed with the ingenuity and generosity of her sister, Water. Pat had the courtesy to ask and the patience to listen. Water spoke, adjusted her course, and went on her way, leaving her human sister with the honor and responsibility to show others how to enter into a personal relationship with the elements that sustain us.

Luminous Web of Interbeing

While we need to make our individual voices and our actions count, we can also call for guidance and inspiration from our ancestors. There are precedents for this reverence and care. There are legends to awaken us and archetypes to guide our steps.

In many indigenous traditions, the feminine face of the Holy One takes the form of a spider that weaves the world into being, affirming our mutual dependence with one another and the planet we share. In the Pueblo Indian tradition of the Rio Grande Valley of northern New Mexico, where I live, her true name is secret, so they refer to her simply as Old Spider Woman. The people of Acoma Pueblo believe that when the One Who Made the World created all that is, he left it unfinished. So he commissioned Old Spider Woman to complete creation. He entrusted her with baskets filled with the necessary ingredients, and she handed the baskets to her sisters, who were blinded at first by the radiance spilling from these sacred vessels. Old Spider Woman taught her sisters the prayers to nurture life, and they sang them to the sun and to the earth. When they were finished praying, their sister told them to look in all directions before taking it upon themselves to rule over creation.

Take a breath and look in all directions before stepping up to mend the world.

In the Hopi tradition of Arizona, she is Spider Grandmother, cocreator and sustainer of the world. It is her task to create life to clothe the naked planet. She molds all living things from the ground, mixing earth with her spit, covering creation with her mantle of wisdom. In the Diné tradition, spread throughout the American Southwest, she is Spider Woman, who sings the web of the universe into being. She teaches us to walk the Beauty Way, seeing and celebrating beauty in all directions, all the time. In the tradition of the ancient Maya of Mexico and Central America, she is Ix Chel, goddess of the moon, water, weaving, and childbirth. One of Ix Chel's titles is Spider's Web Catching the Morning Dew. She is often depicted with a spindle and loom. Like the Diné creator goddess, Ix Chel introduced the art of weaving to the people.

The essence of these spider stories lies in the truth of interconnectedness. When the Great Weaver spins the yarn of physicality and weaves the tapestry of creation, she is fashioning a web in which every link connects to every other link. Everything is vitally, extravagantly interconnected.

Consider the story of Indra's net from the Flower Garland Sutra of Mahayana Buddhism. Indra is a male deity with the feminine task of maintaining the web of interbeing to which we all belong. In his heavenly abode there hangs an exquisite net that stretches infinitely in all directions. A luminous jewel has been placed at the center of each intersection of threads. Each one of these jewels reflects all the others. So not only is the net infinite, but the reflection of the net extends to infinity. Just as tikkun olam anticipated the big bang theory by five hundred years, so too does Indra's net predate the holographic principle in physics by a couple of millennia. Our souls have always understood that everything is interconnected. And radiantly beautiful. And good.

OUR MOTHER, THE EARTH

When Christianity collided with indigenous religions around the world, a kind of nuclear fusion unfolded between the Earth Mother and the Mother of Christ. The apparition known as Our Lady of Guadalupe, from the Valley of Mexico, is a particularly potent example. This hybrid of Mother Mary and Tonantzin, the Mother of the Corn in the Aztec tradition, appeared on the exact spot where the Nahuatl people had been worshiping the fertility goddess for millennia, and she spoke first to an indigenous farmer in his own language. Her skin was dark like their own, yet her features were European. She wore the traditional pre-Columbian maternity sash and also a mantle of stars, like the Virgin Mary. She made it clear that she was the Mother of All People and that her task and her delight was to love us, to give us shelter, to comfort our hearts, and to protect us.

The appearance of Our Lady in the sixteenth century in the Valley of Mexico coincided with the height of the Spanish Conquest, when the colonizers were systematically eradicating indigenous culture, murdering dissenters, and strangling the rights of the native people. The tender mercy of Mother Mary alchemically melded with the fierce power of the Mother of the Corn, and a glorious advocate emerged. Our Lady of Guadalupe bypassed the fear and suspicion engendered by the oppressors and offered a reconciling love that has continued as a wellspring of support for the people of Latin America for five centuries. Some refer to her as the Goddess of the Americas. For many believers, she is as important as Jesus, if not more so (though most Catholics would not proclaim this out loud). Her image—standing on a crescent moon, encircled by stars—adorns the walls of barrios and the hoods of pickup trucks, roadside shrines and flower gardens, from Los Angeles to the Yucatan.

In the Andes, Mother Earth is known as Pachamama. Like Tonantzin, she was both revered and feared by the ancient people. When the *conquistadores* (Spanish colonizers) imposed Christianity, Pachamama absorbed some of the qualities of Mother Mary, fusing the wild and benevolent aspects of the Great Mother into a single, generous Earth goddess. Unlike the concept of tikkun olam, predicated on the assumption that the world is torn and we need to mend it, the Andean peoples of South America see the universe as a place of lavish abundance, symbolized by the ever-giving mother of us all, Pachamama.

Still, we belong to a cycle of reciprocity, and we must not take more than we offer. The people of the Andes pay close attention to the needs of Pachamama and engage in elaborate rituals to give back for the abundance she lavishes on us all. My friend Annamarie, who leads women's groups to the Peruvian Andes, tells me about the principle and practice of *ayni*, "the reciprocal exchange of living energy that occurs through giving offerings and receiving gifts from Mother Earth [Pachamama]." The indigenous Andean people are taught from a young age that all living beings are connected and that we must dwell in balance with the Earth and each other. This is not so much a suggestion about how to live but a recognition of natural law: all life seeks to be in a state of harmony and will inexorably flow toward equilibrium.

The people of the Andes recognize that we all come from Pachamama and that everything belongs to her. "We breathe *her* air," Annamarie says. "We drink *her* water and live on *her* land. The people take care of *her* animals, which feed and clothe them." They revere the Mother by making offerings. When a baby is born, the family will wrap her in a blanket and place her in a shallow hole so that Pachamama can hold her first. Sick children are placed in a similar hole so that Pachamama can heal them. In the spirit of ayni, the Andean people offer simple gifts on a daily basis: seashells, flowers, feathers, candy.

Along with her Andean sisters and brothers, Annamarie believes that by voluntarily simplifying our lives and sending love and gratitude to Pachamama, we can meaningfully contribute to the healing of the Earth. "As humans move into the practice of ayni," she tells me, "Pachamama will thrive again."

And so we of the Global North question our inherited Western values, which are largely masculine values, that encourage us to acquire and hoard whatever we can before it's gone. We give ourselves over to the more feminine impulse to share resources, share wisdom, share joy. We plant ourselves again and again in the fertile soil of our connection with Mother Earth. We walk lightly. We give thanks.

HILDEGARD

The medieval Rhineland visionary Hildegard of Bingen got away with worshiping Mother Earth in the midst of running her Benedictine abbey because she showed her to us through the church-approved lens of Mother Mary and Mother Sophia. Otherwise she would likely have been marked as a pagan and condemned as a heretic. According to Hildegard, it is Mary who spins earthly matter into being and weaves it together with the heavens so that all of creation is interpenetrated with the sacred. In Hildegard's theology, Mary merges with Sophia, Mother Wisdom, who dips one wing to earth while the other soars to heaven and, in her ecstatic flight, quickens life. She imbues us with yearning for her. This is not heresy; it's orthodoxy. It may have taken a thousand years for the church to see the light (the "Living Light," as Hildegard referred to the Divine), but Hildegard was finally canonized in the early twenty-first century, and proclaimed "Doctor of the Church"—a rare honor bestowed on those saints who meaningfully contribute to Roman Catholic theology.

Hildegard was smitten with the creator and enamored by every element of creation. Her mysticism is intimate—erotic, even. She coined the term *viriditas* to evoke the lush, extravagant, moist, and verdant quality of the Divine, manifesting as the "greening power" that permeates all that is. This life-giving energy is imbued with a distinctly feminine quality.

> The earth is at the same time
> mother,
> she is mother of all that is natural,
> mother of all that is human.
> She is the mother of all,
> for contained in her
> are the seeds of all.   **HILDEGARD OF BINGEN**

For Hildegard, the Son may be the incarnation of the Holy One, but the Mother forms the very stuff from which the Word of God issues forth into the world. The mystical heart of all the world's religions affirms the profoundly feminine understanding of *panentheism*: that is, all the particles of the universe are infused with the substance of the Divine; God both interpenetrates the universe and is greater than all that is.

SITA

Mother Sita is one of the most beloved goddesses of Hindu mythology. Few of her devotees, however, remember that she is, in many ways, an avatar of Mother Earth. Sita is born of Mother Earth, found as an infant in a furrow where her adopted father was plowing his field. She followed her husband, Lord Ram, into exile in the forest, where they lived in simplicity, close to the earth, for fourteen years. There, she communicated with animals, crafted herbal remedies, and sensed climate shifts.

What most people think they know of Sita comes from the classic Hindu epic the Ramayana, which tells the famous story of Sita's abduction by Ravana, the evil ten-headed demon. Ravana glimpses Sita as he rides his chariot through the sky, desires her on the spot, and carries her off to his demon abode across the sea on the island of Lanka. An epic battle unfolds in which the humble monkey king, Hanuman, rescues Sita and she is restored to her rightful place by Ram's side.

The Ramayana is an iconic tale of love and separation, of languishing and homecoming. It serves as an archetype for the reunification of the feminine and masculine faces of the Godhead. It also relegates Sita to the status of chaste and obedient spouse and reinforces the stereotype of the helpless female. My friend Dena Merriam, who has spent a lifetime studying Hindu texts and meditating on their meaning, has a different take on Sita's story. She says that Sita was not Ravana's victim but rather the architect of her own fate. Sita willingly took on the karma of her incarnation to help turn the consciousness of humanity back to right relationship with the Earth. Nor was Sita merely Ram's devotee; she was a full and equal participant in the teaching of the dharma (spiritual law).

Sita is all about connection with nature. At the end of her life, she was weary from the many tribulations of her incarnation, including a painful rupture with her beloved Ram, who, imagining his wife's violation at the hands of the evil Ravana, eventually cast her off. Sita returned to the arms of Mother Earth, who broke herself open and, taking Sita's hand, lovingly received her.

Our experiences of embodiment may not always correspond with idealized images of holiness, but these preconceptions derive from masculine standards of perfection. Such paradigms have caused great harm, and they are no longer valid. I invite you to abandon your efforts to fix yourself and instead reclaim your innate beauty and worth as a luminous cell in the body of Mother Earth.

deepening

Sit quietly, with your eyes closed, and allow your mind to explore the breadth and depth of the degradation of Mother Earth. Refrain from either pushing away the pain or translating it into self-righteous rage. Allow yourself to linger in the places that cause you discomfort.

Now identify one particular issue that most deeply troubles you, either close to home or in a remote region of the planet. Be present with this reality for a few minutes.

Ask yourself what practical steps you could take to alleviate some of this suffering in the world. Resolve to take action in some small or large way. Follow through. And if you feel overwhelmed, remember, you are not alone. Join your energy with the energy of others. And consider what Mother Teresa said: "Not all of us can do great things, but we can do small things with great love."

Your action may be as simple as declining to use plastic straws, knowing how discarded straws are severely disrupting the ecosystems of the world's oceans. Maybe you will choose to bike to work one day a week, lightening your carbon footprint and contributing to your own fitness. Try reading one new article on climate change each week and use social media to educate the people to whom you are connected.

Bring down your colors
Break open your box of song
Beauty lifts us up

9

MAKING A JOYFUL NOISE

Creativity and the Arts

opening

When you were a child, you knew yourself to be
cocreator of the universe. But little by little you
forgot who you were. When you were a child,
everything was about color. Now you pick black as
your automatic font color, because that is the coin
of the realm. When you were a child, you made up
songs. You don't sing much anymore; you lecture, or
you yell, or you keep a safe silence. When you were
a child, you traveled from place to place by dancing,
and now you cultivate stillness, which is great, but
you are forgetting how to move to the music of your
soul. You can hardly even hear that inner music over
the clamor of all your obligations.

Reclaim your wild creativity. I know it's dangerous.
When you allow yourself to become a conduit for
Shakti (primordial cosmic energy), she enters like light
and everything becomes illuminated. She fits you like
a second skin, and you feel everything—pervasive bliss,
deep ache. She makes you hungry, fills you up, makes
you drowsy, keeps you awake all night. She arouses

praise and moves you to lament. She is the sacred taking the ordinary hostage. You cannot resist her.

Of course you are afraid of what might happen if you were to lift the lid off that box. A thousand beautiful things might come tumbling out and take over your life. You could be consumed by the urge to compose a libretto or paint a mural and lose track of your responsibilities. You are smart to be wary of opening the cage to your sleeping artistic impulses. They are likely to come roaring forth like flames and take your orderly life to the ground. Next thing you know you'll be bursting into song at parent-teacher meetings or doodling all over your tax returns. What if you were to follow the visions that fill your head and heart, begging to be manifest through your hands, and you ended up neglecting your children's breakfast?

It is not always so risky to make art. You don't have to dedicate the whole of your life to Shakti's impulse to create. Beauty blooms in tight spaces. You are not too busy or too poor or too independent to learn to throw earthenware pots or play the drums. When you make time for beauty, the universe miraculously expands to welcome it. You find yourself picking up the guitar you hadn't tuned since college and noodling around. Suddenly you can play "House of the Rising Sun" again, and it sounds better than ever, seasoned as it is by all those years of unfortunate choices and sweet suffering. Instead of watching the nightly news, you compile all those freewrites you have scribbled in assorted notebooks and in the margins of takeout menus. You type them up and watch them bloom into a poetry garden.

Lo and behold, you still balance the checkbook, hang the laundry, and help your kids with their math assignments (even if you didn't love math yourself).

Yes, you are worthy of art making. Dispense with the hierarchy in your head that silences your own creative voice by suggesting that you could never be a Picasso or a Puccini and so you might as well not even bother painting or composing. Of course you could never be a master like those masters. They were men, and it is men who set the stage for artistic mastery, just as it is men who built the altars of the world's religions and then discouraged women from joining them there. It is not only your birthright to create, it is your true nature. The world will be healed when you take up your brush and shake your body and sing your heart out. Shakti, the feminine, the dynamic nature of reality, is dying to take you for a spin.

The Alchemy of Art

A miraculous event unfolds when we throw the lead of our personal story into the transformative flames of creativity. Our hardship is transmuted into something golden. With that gold we heal ourselves and redeem the world. As with any spiritual practice, this creative alchemy requires a leap of faith. When we show up to make art, we need to first get still enough to hear what wants to be expressed through us, and then we need to step out of the way and let it. We must be willing to abide in a space of not knowing before we can settle into knowing. Such a space is sacred. It is liminal, and it's numinous. It is frightening and enlivening. It demands no less than everything, and it gives back tenfold.

There is a vital connection between creativity and mysticism. To engage with the creative impulse is to agree to take a voyage into the heart of the Mystery. Creativity bypasses the discursive mind and delivers us to the source of our being. When we allow ourselves to be a conduit for creative energy, we experience direct apprehension of that energy. We become a channel for grace. To make art is to make love with the sacred. It is a naked encounter, authentic and risky, vulnerable and erotically charged.

The muse rarely behaves the way we would like her to, and yet every artist knows she cannot be controlled. Artistic self-expression necessitates periods of quietude in which it appears that nothing is happening. Like a tree in winter whose roots are doing important work deep inside the dark earth, the creative process needs fallow time. We have to incubate inspiration. We need empty spaces for musing and preparing, experimenting and reflecting. Society does not value its artists, partly because of the apparent lack of productivity that comes with the creative life. This societal emphasis on goods and services is an artifact of the male drive to erect and protect, to engineer and execute, to produce and control. Art begins with receptivity. Every artist, in a way, is feminine, just as every artist is a mystic. And a political creature. Making art can be a subversive act, an act of resistance against the deadening lure of consumption, an act of unbridled peacemaking disguised as a poem or a song or an abstract rendering of an aspen leaf swirling in a stream.

The part of our brains with which we navigate the challenges of the everyday world is uneasy in the unpredictable sphere of art making. We cannot squeeze ourselves through the eye of the needle to reach the land of wild creativity whilst saddled to the frontal cortex, whose job it is to evaluate external circumstances and regulate appropriate behavior. Creativity has a habit of defying good sense. I am not arguing, however, that the intellect has no place in the creative enterprise. The most intelligent people I know are artists and musicians. Their finely tuned minds are always grappling with some creative conundrum, trying to find ways to translate the music they hear in the concert hall of their heads into some intelligible form that others can grasp and appreciate.

What a creative life demands is that we take risks. They may be calculated risks; they may yield entrepreneurial fruits, or they may simply enrich our own lives. Creative risk taking might not turn our life upside down but, rather, might right the drifting ship of our soul. When we make ourselves available for the inflow of

Shakti, we accept not only her generative power but also her ability to destroy whatever stands in the way of our full aliveness.

You do not always have to suffer for art. You are not required to sacrifice everything for beauty. The creative life can be quietly gratifying. The thing is to allow ourselves to become a vessel for a work of art to come through and allow that work to guide our hands. Once we do, we are assenting to a sacred adventure. We are saying yes to the transcendent and embodied presence of the holy.

SARASWATI

Picture this: A luminous goddess seated on a white lotus blossom beside a flowing river. In one of her four arms she holds a book—the ancient Vedas, the source of perennial knowledge and symbol of the power of literature to transform consciousness. In another hand she holds a *mala*, a string of 108 crystal beads, the source of deep concentration and symbol of the power of meditation to generate one-pointed awareness. In another hand she holds a vessel filled with sacred water, the source of purification and symbol of the power of creativity to refine wisdom to its essence. In her fourth hand she holds a vina, a stringed musical instrument, the source of perfection for all the arts, symbol of the power of music to awaken the heart.

She is Saraswati, and she's my muse. This Hindu goddess is all about the flow of creative energy and clarity of expression. She is passionate and focused, elegant and lucid. She is unadorned, far more interested in the process of creating beauty than in being an object of beauty herself. Sometimes she is accompanied by a swan, symbol of discernment, or a peacock, symbol of grace. She emerged from the mouth of Brahma, the creator, when he wished to create meaning from the formless chaos of nonexistence. This makes Saraswati cocreator of the universe. She is Brahma's consort, yes, but Brahma is also Sarsawati's consort. Their love play unfolds in the microcosm of our souls.

I have a small statue of the goddess beside my writing desk to help endow me with creative flow. I also have a host of other inspiring feminine wisdom beings, such as the Pueblo Indian storyteller, a clay figurine of a grandmother with her mouth open and many children in her arms as she tells them the legends of their people. The storyteller figure is a modern expression of the perennial oral tradition, in which we simultaneously safeguard ancestral wisdom and meet it anew in our own times, our own communities, our own bodies.

ONE OF EACH

My friend Azima sees creativity as a sacred stream that flows above our heads. Occasionally we are able to connect to it and bring it down to earth through music or painting, poetry or dance. The forms it takes are exquisitely various, but the source is One.

She should know. Azima wins the contest for practicing the most artistic forms, and engaging them all with great mastery, in service to the One. Born in Bulgaria under the Communist regime, Azima studied piano at the National Academy of Music in Sofia, which opened the way for her to escape oppression, and she continued her studies in Rome, where she also began performing to great acclaim. Swiftly gaining a reputation as a virtuoso pianist, Azima was recognized with multiple awards for her brilliance, including a prize for "virtuosity with distinction" from the Geneva Conservatory of Music. She accepted teaching positions throughout Europe. Eventually she settled in London, married a Scottish clan chief, had two children with him, and directed a chamber music festival for ten years on the Isle of Skye. Azima still lives in London, but she regularly travels the world, riding camels in the Sahara and praying in silence in the Sinai, creating painting diaries in South India and writing her memoirs in New Mexico.

Like the story of every mystic I know, it was only when the seams of Azima's carefully stitched life began to unravel that the holy mystery infiltrated the fabric and everything turned inside out, leaving her with a soul on fire and an unquenchable urge to create. Following her divorce, Azima continued playing piano but began writing and painting as well. She discovered the work of the great medieval Sufi master Jalaluddin Rumi (or, as Azima puts it, Rumi found her). Then she collaborated with a native Persian speaker to translate Rumi's poetry into a fresh, accessible English that is deeply steeped in the mystical aspects of his teachings. This intimacy with the ecstatic poet led Azima to create a musical group called Lovers of Rumi. They gave concerts all over Europe, weaving short musical movements by Bach, Scriabin, and Brahms (played by Azima) with the poetry of Rumi. Many different people across the religious and cultural spectrum read the poems.

Azima found me after my second book, a translation of Teresa of Ávila's *The Interior Castle*, was published in the United Kingdom. She sensed we would resonate with each other and took the risk of reaching out. A holy conversation unfolded, charged with energy, blessing my life with the kind of soul companionship I had rarely experienced. We wrote each other long emails, sharing our broken hearts and our life stories. I was only a couple of years out from the firestorm of my daughter's death, and my heart still had no skin. I wasn't interested in anything less than full and authentic connection with other human beings on a path of transformation in love.

Over the years, Azima and I have visited each other's worlds, sharing music and poetry, food and Sufi practices. In between, we tend the thread of our connection with varying degrees of communication and silence. A watercolor Azima made for me of the opening page of Rumi's multivolume poem *The Masnavi* hangs above my writing desk, and her icon of Christ holding up his hand in a mudra of blessing is propped on the bookshelf behind me.

What strikes me most about Azima is how elegantly she embodies that which my own soul knew as a young girl yet had trouble pulling off: each of the creative arts are different languages with which to praise the Divine, and they are all interconnected.

Becoming Beauty

As you may have gathered, I was never at home in the academic world. I did well in college, but only because I worked my ass off, spending most of my stint in exile, well beyond my right-brained comfort zone. Somewhere midway through my graduate studies in philosophy, I had an epiphany. I was not interested in either the logical validity or the utility of ideas; I was drawn to their aesthetic value. When an argument was presented with passion and literary power, my whole body responded, and this visceral resonance constituted agreement. This was nothing to be ashamed of!

"You cannot step in the same river twice" (Heraclitus). "Whereof we cannot speak, we must remain silent" (Wittgenstein). "God is dead" (Nietzsche). Fine! Most of the material we read and wrote about was generated by DWM (Dead White Men), but my radar skirted their cognitive credentials and honed in on their feminine hearts.

This aesthetic sensibility was partly an artifact of the way I was raised. My dad read math books for pleasure. He swooned in the face of the elegance of certain theorems. As other fathers might quote the Bible, he would also recite from the modernist poem "The Love Song of J. Alfred Prufrock" by T. S. Eliot, lines such as "Let us go then, you and I, / When the evening is spread out against the sky. . . ." My mom painted with oils, drew with pastels, sculpted with metals and stone. When we were growing up, she played the guitar and sang folk ballads. Even today, moved by a coyote drinking from her garden fountain or news of a vast network of Mayan city-states discovered in Guatemala, my mom's response is to compose poetry, short stories, lyrical essays.

My parents did not attend synagogue and never stepped foot in a church, but they bowed at the altar of the arts. They belonged to the cult of Dostoevsky, who proclaimed that beauty would save the world. Yet I also learned from my family that beauty is not limited to that which is pleasing. Art can be jarring or dissonant, offensive or haphazard. It disrupts the dominant paradigm and unloosens the chains of conventionality. This chaotic quality, too, is in the wildly creative nature of Shakti.

My own relationship with beauty has never been one of detached appreciation. It is a direct encounter in which the subject-object distinction becomes irrelevant. Nor is my connection with the beautiful limited to the arts, although it is best evoked through the arts. Stopping for a moment to catch the call of a mourning dove in my driveway transports me. I forget to open my car door and get in and drive to the post office, as planned. All my other senses start to flower. I smell the high desert yearning for snow. The blue sky bends to touch the crown of my head. Time inhales, and I am suspended in that space between breaths. Beauty commands silence and stillness. It invites the momentary dissolution of self-identity. What a relief!

FORM AND FREEDOM

Chiyo-ni was born in eighteenth-century Japan, just after the death of Basho, a master of the incredibly brief form of poetry known as haiku. Haiku is precise. It conforms to an exact syllabic count: the first line has five syllables, the second has seven, and the third has five. Within that container the poet's wings expand in all directions, touching the ordinary and rendering it extraordinary. There is freedom in form.

Just as women were not historically permitted to be rabbis or priests, astronomers or philosopher-kings, there are almost no female haiku poets of Chiyo-ni's time. Yet Chiyo-ni defied convention as a very young girl and began composing poetry at age seven. By the time she was seventeen, her poems were admired all over Japan. While Basho was an important influence on Chiyo-ni, she swiftly developed a voice of her own. Her poetry exudes brisk simplicity and unclouded vision. She observed the ordinary world with such loving attention that it could not resist revealing its hidden treasures.

I came across her most famous poem, "The Morning Glory," many years ago in D.T. Suzuki's ecstatic essay about it.

> The morning glory!
> It has taken the well bucket.
> I must ask elsewhere for water.

Here is a woman so available for the encounter with beauty that seeing the delicate flower momentarily arrests her capacity to function, Suzuki tells us. Returning to her senses, rather than dare to disentangle the vine from the bucket, she leaves it undisturbed and goes to a neighbor's well to complete her chore. In three quiet lines of verse, Chiyo-ni expresses the amplitude of feminine spirituality: finding the sacred in the ordinary and praising it with the fullness of her being.

Chiyo-ni, who insisted on living a life of simplicity and humility, is recognized as one of the most important figures in the history of Japanese literature. She spoke with candor and playfulness about the experience of being a woman. She writes of women planting rice with their hair in disarray, forgoing painted lips for clear spring water, airing out their hearts along with their kimonos.

I have always flourished within certain formal boundaries myself. Growing up as an artistic child in the counterculture, with its emphasis on free expression, I often detected a subtle criticism of my drawings. My impulse toward exactitude was seen as regimented. "Why don't you color outside the lines once in a while?" my mom would challenge me. When I learned to play the guitar, I kept close to the arpeggios and fingerpicking patterns I practiced between lessons. I studied folk dancing and South Indian classical dance, reveling in precision of movement. When I was sixteen, I moved out of the house I shared with my teacher and his family in Mendocino, and I paid the rent for my one-room cabin in the redwoods by designing specialized logos for business cards. Later, I made my way through college as a scientific illustrator, rendering elaborately shaded fossil bones and decorative potsherds entirely of dots.

I thought there was something wrong with me. *I should be more improvisational. I should dance like no one's watching, strum with a loose wrist, sing scat, layer my canvas with broad brushstrokes and no agenda.* But over the years, as with all aspects of my life, I have come to accept my artistic proclivities and embrace them. I am someone who appreciates structure, such as the haiku's strict five-seven-five syllable count. I compose haiku in my sleep and wake feeling satisfied. I memorize the lyrics to songs in multiple languages and take joy in singing along with the artists who record them. Safely held in the vessel of form, my soul unfurls and ventures into the beautiful wilderness. My adherence to convention does not preclude my wild creativity: it gives it a platform from which to launch.

The way of the feminine is about the movement from formlessness into form, from quietude to expression, a pouring of the waters of the void into the ground of being.

deepening

Create an art piece as an offering to the Divine Feminine. It can be in any form: painting, drawing, sculpture, pottery, sewing, weaving, poetry, prose, theater, dance, music, cooking, gardening—whatever captures your imagination and engages your wild creativity. You may work on it for as long as you need to, but make sure to share it with at least one other person when you're done.

Goddess of mercy
Show me the way back home to Love
Womb of compassion

10

FORGIVING

The Art of Mercy

opening

I'm sorry. I'm so sorry that I broke your heart,
that I was too demanding of your approval, that I
forgot to put your name in my acknowledgments.
I'm sorry I ignored you at the poetry reading and
didn't bother to correct the perception that I don't
care about you. I'm sorry I didn't attend your
concert, your wedding, your funeral. I'm sorry I
talked too much at the dinner party. I'm sorry I
was so quiet. I'm sorry I gave you a low grade on
your midterm exam. I'm sorry I was a mother
who put my relationships with men ahead of
my children. I'm sorry I was the kind of mother
who hovered like a blimp and smothered
you. I'm sorry I interpreted your rejection as
rejection, rather than as the cry for love that it
really was.

I forgive you. I forgive you for dying young.
I forgive you for drinking too much and acting
like an asshole. I forgive you for talking about
me behind my back. I forgive you for running

over my neighbor and her daughter who were out for a walk. I forgive you for leaving your girlfriend when she told you she was pregnant. I forgive you for accusing me of being arrogant when I was just excited. I forgive you for not seeing me.

I forgive you for being blind to your own shadow, for your participation in institutionalized racism, misogyny, heteronormativity. I forgive you for your anti-Semitic jokes and your Islamophobic remarks. I forgive you for lobbying for ownership of assault weapons, amassing a nuclear arsenal, building a wall to keep out people of color and separate children from their parents. I forgive you for genocide against the indigenous peoples of this and every other continent. I forgive you for the Holocaust that exterminated my ancestors like bugs. I forgive you for the slave trade, for sex trafficking, for treating garbage collectors like garbage. I forgive you for putting profits ahead of people, technology ahead of clean air and water, head ahead of heart.

Forgiving you was the best thing I ever did. Forgiving you set the bird of my heart winging through the universe.

Quan Yin

She is the bodhisattva of compassion, the embodiment of loving-kindness, the personification of mercy. She Who Hears the Cries of the World; She Who Sees the Wounds of the World. She is the incarnation of the Buddha of compassion, who had the option of merging into the boundless ocean of Nirvana and chose instead to return to the wheel of samsara (births, deaths, rebirths) in feminine form, as Quan Yin, to comfort and awaken all beings until every being is free from suffering.

It is said that Quan Yin was born a woman, Miao Shan, and that, like so many legendary female saints, she flowered in the face of persecution. Her parents wanted a boy child, and they did their best to get rid of Miao Shan as soon as possible. In the meantime, they put her to work doing the most arduous household tasks. Not only did her labors fail to bring Miao Shan down, but she drew the attention of the forest creatures, who joined forces to help her. The mice threaded her needles, the rabbits swept the courtyard, the deer split kindling for the cook fire.

When it came time for her to be married off, Miao Shan informed her parents that she preferred to become a nun. They refused. She insisted. Finally her father sent her to a convent of his own choosing, but only after striking a deal with the abbess that Miao Shan be assigned the grungiest duties so she would be discouraged from monastic life.

Miao Shan was appointed to the convent hospice, where she was meant to tend infectious wounds, clean up all manner of bodily fluids, and prepare corpses for burial. This job, of course, was perfect for Miao Shan. She not only cared for her patients' physical needs, she also loved them through their deepest suffering. She sang to them and sat with them in silence. And when they died, she accompanied them to the otherworld to make sure they were safe.

When her father found out that Miao Shan was thriving where he hoped she would capitulate, he ordered her execution. As the henchman raised his ax over her head, Miao Shan looked into his eyes and forgave him for what he was about to do. She assured him that he would not bear the karmic burden for this deed. Unable to carry out an act of violence upon such an angelic being, he threw down his ax, which shattered into a thousand pieces. Miao Shan was swept up in a pearly mist and transported to a nearby island, where she spent the rest of her life in meditation. When she died, she became Quan Yin, embodiment of selfless service and sweet mercy.

Do not be fooled. Miao Shan's humility was not compliant; it was subversive! Quan Yin's compassion is not indulgent; it is subversive! It invites us to lay down our weapons and open our hearts. The tender attributes of the feminine do not render her weak and ineffectual. They glorify her. Our vulnerability is our strength. Our capacity to forgive is our superpower.

Making Amends

Every wisdom tradition on the planet emphasizes that compassion is the quintessence of the holy. The Arabic word *rahim*, found in the opening lines of the Qur'an and repeated many times a day in the *salat* (daily prayers), means "compassion." *Rahim* is also the word for "womb." Forgiveness is the very face of the Divine Feminine. Each time we allow mercy to enter the shattered spaces of our hearts, we participate in the divine nature. To forgive ourselves is to forge a contract with the Divine Mother: I will mirror you in my own soul. Yet this is not so much a decision as an allowing. It is grace.

Women have a tendency to overapologize. Not all women, of course. But many of us have been conditioned to avoid taking up space in this world, expressing our opinions, asking for what we want. We are compelled to beg forgiveness for being and may use this compulsion as a kind of preemptive technique, accusing ourselves before we can be accused and thereby escaping condemnation. While we may find this habit of apologizing for every little thing annoying in others, it's harder to catch our own self-deprecating behaviors. We would never speak to a beloved child the way we talk to ourselves sometimes in the middle of the night when we can't help rewinding the tape of our lives and blaming ourselves for a thousand missteps. We wouldn't even treat a stranger so harshly. What would happen if we cultivated tenderness toward our own broken being? What revolution would unfold if we embraced the teachings of the mystics and practiced cherishing ourselves?

Of course, making amends is almost always a vital spiritual practice. Every tradition has rituals for taking a moral inventory, asking for and receiving forgiveness. They all encourage us to engage in concrete action to rectify any damage caused by our shortcomings while acknowledging that we are likely to mess up again and offering techniques for growing our consciousness around the kinds of behaviors that caused us to miss the mark. The vulnerability such practices engender is in itself holy ground. We soften our grip on the separate self and leave the ego undefended, affirming our interdependence with all beings and finding our footing in the human condition.

Treasure Yourself

My friend Ondrea Levine is a prophet of self-forgiveness. Beloved partner of the late Stephen Levine, revered for his pioneering work with conscious dying, Ondrea is a powerful teacher in her own right. Her teaching is deceptively simple and cuts like a diamond through our calcified self-hatred: *Treasure yourself.*

There is often a sense of peace that descends on our hearts when we cultivate the courage to forgive. We are tangibly blessed even as we bless others with our mercy. Yet it can be easier to absolve someone who wronged you, Ondrea points out, than to forgive yourself. Most of us are way harder on ourselves than we are on others. We'd sooner pardon a violent criminal whose childhood, as it turns out, was riddled with parental neglect and abuse than give ourselves a break for waking up in a bad mood and snapping at our children.

The unfinished business with which most people die, Ondrea continues, is the work of forgiveness, mostly forgiveness of themselves. Ondrea told me how much she cherishes the private conversations she's had with many people as they were dying, in which they entrusted her with their deepest secrets. They needed a loving person to bear witness to these soul burdens they carried so that they could lay them down before they died. Sharing their hearts with Ondrea helped them to forgive themselves. But the exchange was not one-way. These intimate moments with the dying bestowed gifts of love Ondrea says she will keep with her until the day she dies.

A few years ago, Ondrea launched something she calls "The Apology Page" on the Levine Talks website. This is a public space where people can post anonymously, confessing the transgressions that cloud their conscience and blight their relationships. "It seems to be a very good idea as a means for tilting the shared heart and letting it pour into the ocean of compassion," Stephen and Ondrea wrote at the top of the web page. "If you were told you were completely forgiven for everything you have ever done, what is it in the heart that rejects that self-mercy? Treasure Yourselves."

The apologies range from what may appear to be minor offences, such as envy, to significant betrayals, such as a spouse admitting to an affair. "I apologize to my mother for thinking daily about killing myself," one person writes. Some, like this one, carry remorse about actions they committed years ago: "I am sorry that, as a teenager, around fifteen years old, when I was babysitting, I left the baby alone, asleep in the house to go to a dance for a few hours." Some recognize the ways in which they have caused harm to their own dear selves: "I apologize to myself for repressing my femininity, my desires and my feelings. I apologize to myself for believing I was valuable only if I was strong, clever and showed no feelings. I apologize to myself for striving for spiritual perfection and disregarding my humanness."

There is a soft, cool breeze flowing through "The Apology Page." It feels like a safe grotto where we can rest. Glimpsing the ways other people flagellate themselves, just as we do, can generate a couple of healing outcomes. It helps us see our participation in the universal predicament—that we are neither terminally special nor uniquely flawed—and that we belong to the human family. And the simple act of naming the ways we have missed the mark helps recalibrate our hearts and line us back up with our most loving intentions.

ALL WILL BE WELL AND ALL WILL BE WELL

The medieval English anchoress Julian of Norwich bequeathed us a radically optimistic theology. She had no problem admitting that human beings have a tendency to go astray. We rupture relationships, dishonor the Divine, make unfortunate choices, and try to hide our faults. And yet, Julian insists, "All will be well and all will be well and every kind of thing shall be well."

Take that in.

This assertion is meant to penetrate the fog of our despair and wake us up. She does not simply state, "Everything's going to be okay." Like God calling the biblical prophets by name, Julian repeats her declaration three times—most emphatically the third: *All will be well and all will be well and every kind of thing shall be well.* She does not ask us to engage in a spiritual bypass by relegating everything that unfolds to the will of God, calling it perfect against all evidence to the contrary. She squarely faces the inevitability that we will miss the mark and that there is wickedness in this world. Even so, she is convinced that the nature of the Divine is loving-kindness, and she wants us to absorb this into every fiber of our being.

In her mystical masterwork *The Showings,* Julian shares that she used to obsess about sin. She couldn't figure out why God, who is all-powerful, wouldn't have eliminated our negative proclivities when he made the world. "If he had left sin out of creation, it seemed to me, all would be well." But what God-the-Mother showed Julian in a near-death vision was that all shall be well anyway. Not in spite of our transgressions but because of them.

Julian unpacks this for us. In doing so she dispenses with the whole concept of sin and replaces it with love. "I believe that sin has no substance," Julian writes, "not a particle of being." While sin itself has no existential value, it has impact. It causes pain. It is the pain that has substance.

But mercy is swiftly forthcoming. It is immediately available. Inexorable! It is frankly rude of us to doubt that all will be well (and all will be well and every kind of thing shall be well). "When he said these gentle words," Julian writes, speaking of God-the-Mother, "he showed me that he does not have one iota of blame for me, or for any other person. So, wouldn't it be unkind of me to blame God for my transgressions since he does not blame me?" The merciful nature of God renders the whole blame game obsolete. Besides, in her visions, Julian saw that we are perfectly protected. We're bound to do things we regret, whether or not we intend to, but we each carry a spark of the Holy One inside us, and this can never be extinguished. In fact, it is when we stumble that the Divine looks most tenderly upon us. Our vulnerability is beautiful to God-the-Mother.

Suffering is a purifying fire, a blessing in itself. Julian predicts that when this life is over we will understand that there is no punishment, only grace. We have already paid for our transgressions through the pain we endured as a consequence of our negative actions. In fact, we will be rewarded in direct proportion to the severity of our errors. This may seem counterintuitive, but why would a loving God, Julian asks, hold us accountable for that which we have already offered to the flames of remorse? Not only would God never allow our souls to suffer for the actions we have already accounted for in this life, but each soul is so precious to God that when she brings us home to herself she offers us the seat of honor at her own table.

For those of us who do not subscribe to a belief in some perfect afterworld but, rather, are focused on making things better right here on Earth, this teaching may feel disconnected. But what Julian is saying, with heartbreaking compassion, is that we cannot know this now, from our limited, pain-drenched perspective. Yet eventually we will awaken to the truth that we are unconditionally adored by God, so that in the end, "We will clearly see in God all the secrets that are hidden from us now. Then none of us will be moved in any way to say, 'Lord, if only things had been different, all would have been well.' Instead, we shall proclaim in one voice, 'Beloved One, may you be blessed, because it is so: all is well.'"

Our task is to embody these "heavenly realms" here and now, in our relationships, in our communities, in our bedraggled and beautiful hearts.

Restorative Justice

It is no surprise that many indigenous wisdom practices echo feminine values. Native cultures are generally earth-based, and the Earth is honored as our Mother. When there is violence or discord within the collective sphere, certain tribes in Canada, the United States, Australia, and New Zealand (and undoubtedly in many other regions less documented) will gather in a circle, and the members will take turns speaking from the heart about how the incident touched them and what they think might be done to mend the torn fabric of community.

There are so many things about this that feel feminine to me: gathering in a circle, giving space for each voice to be heard and valued, emphasizing healing over punishing. It's about rebuilding relationships.

As a result of the measurable benefits of restorative justice circles among indigenous communities, some nonindigenous groups have taken up this native wisdom teaching. In the classroom and the courtroom, restorative justice methods are being applied to a range of violations, from petty theft to rape, from able-bodied people parking in spots designated for the disabled (so they won't be late to football practice or some such reason) to fatal collisions caused by drunk drivers.

Here's how it works. When a crime has been committed, everyone impacted by the incident comes together in a circle. Each person affected has the opportunity to speak directly to the person responsible for the violation, sharing how they were hurt by the offender's action. The person who committed the crime also has a chance to speak. They can apologize, express their own pain and sorrow for what they did, and may begin developing a concrete plan to restore wholeness to the community. Unlike the punitive model practiced in most Western courts, restorative justice is about repairing harm. It speaks to the whole person; it addresses and heals the soul. The philosophy underlying this process is that when someone violates the rights of an individual, they are damaging the fabric of the entire circle.

One of the most powerful experiences I've ever had—in a lifetime overflowing with powerful experiences—was sitting in a restorative justice circle. I was there in the capacity of grief counselor to a woman whose sixteen-year-old daughter had been run over by her boyfriend following a fight. They were in the parking lot of a motel where they had been partying.

When the young man entered the room where the session was to take place, his hands cuffed and his feet shackled, he did not make eye contact with anyone gathered there, including his own parents. Even after he was seated, he did not look up. Each person spoke of the ways they were impacted by the event, and at first his face was like stone. But little by little, I saw his body language begin to register what was happening around him. As the girl's basketball buddies spoke and cried, he flinched. His girlfriend's sister, who was pregnant, wept when she expressed that her dead sister would never get to be an auntie or a mom herself. Her stepfather spoke of his helplessness in the face of his wife's grief.

When the mother spoke, she did not cry. She did not hurl hateful accusations. She quietly shared the texture of her days, sleepless nights, tortured dreams, waking to remember all over again that her beautiful, feisty daughter was gone. Then, to the amazement of everyone present, she shifted her focus from her own pain to her daughter's boyfriend. She acknowledged that not only had she lost a child, but that he had lost his girlfriend. She told him that she holds him in prayer and that she might even like to visit him in prison to see how he's doing. She hoped this tragedy would inspire him to return to his community and teach boys about nonviolence. As this mighty mama shared her heart, I watched the young man's eyes fill with tears. Soon he was openly weeping. And then we were all crying: her family, his family, the district attorney, and the assistant DA. Me.

When it was my turn to speak, I encouraged the young man to use his prison sentence as a monastic opportunity—to pray and meditate, to read spiritual literature and keep his communication with fellow inmates as respectful and as kind as possible. I offered to send him books that I felt would facilitate a kind of vision quest within the desert of his incarceration: *Dark Night of the Soul* by John of the Cross, *Finding Freedom* by Jarvis Jay Masters, *When Things Fall Apart* by Pema Chödrön.

After everyone had a chance to share how this incident had affected them, a blanket of collective exhaustion laced with tranquility fell over our group and rendered us momentarily mute. The facilitator skillfully allowed us to sit in this scared hush for a few minutes before closing the circle. And then the girl's mom asked if she could hug her daughter's boyfriend. The guards consented. As if in the presence of the Madonna herself, we all made way for her as she crossed the room to where stood the person responsible for her child's death, who was suddenly looking very much like a little boy.

She took him into her arms and began whispering in his ear while stroking his shaved head. His shoulders were trembling, heaving. They stayed that way, pressed together, for a long time.

Then he was led away, back to jail. His sentencing followed later that week, taking into account the transformational fruits of our restorative justice process. The fabric of community had been carefully and collectively rewoven. Not a single one of us would ever be the same.

RECONCILIATION — PERSONAL AND COMMUNAL

While we may comprehend that holding onto resentments is like ingesting spiritual cyanide, it is not easy to let go of the story line of our own wounds. Nor must we. The feminine way is to allow ourselves to feel what we feel, softening and yielding to the reality of the pain, breathing through it like a woman being ripped open by the contractions of labor, and allowing ourselves to birth ourselves anew (again and again). Each time we show up for what is true, our hearts expand and strengthen, increasing our capacity to forgive and be forgiven.

What is true is often nuanced. We are all perpetrators of unconscious bias, and we each get a turn transmuting the poison of victimhood into the medicine of reconciliation. I've lived a life of relative privilege, but I am determined to stand with those on the margins. I have had small tastes of bigotry. Born into a Jewish family only a generation after the Holocaust, I was raised with the visceral reality of the danger of my membership in a particular ethnic minority. "It doesn't matter whether I believe in God or not," my mother used to say (she didn't, FYI). "I would still go into the ovens." The ovens. The gas chambers. This was the symbol of the insanity of a world where people die simply because they are Jewish—or black or brown or gay.

Later, as a hippie kid in the back-to-the-land counter-culture, I felt the judgmental stares of the locals when my barefooted family would schlep our dirty clothes to the Laundromat. I would burn with shame perceiving the consternation on the faces of the retired doctors and their wives when we would visit our grandparents in their fancy Miami Beach high-rise. We didn't look normal, prosperous, predictable. We didn't belong.

Nevertheless, I have come to realize as an adult that my Caucasian skin bequeaths me a pass most people of color will never have, at least not in the dominantly white Western world. I thought I was onto this. I adopted two biracial children, my stepdaughter married a guy from Mexico who has Aztec roots, and my grandchildren are bilingual. I speak fluent Spanish myself, and my connection with Latin culture is so deep that I feel it has shaped my soul. When I glance at the police blotter in our local paper, I often catch myself praying that the perpetrators of the various crimes are Anglo, rather than Hispanic or Native, which would reinforce the bias of my racist neighbors (and then I swiftly apologize to God for wishing harm on anyone ever).

Still, when I look around me, I see my own skin color reflected in film and literature and advertising, in public office and in the university, in yoga classes and meditation groups. The entertainment I enjoy is mostly delivered by white people to white people. The environmental and social activism circles I convene or participate in are largely comprised of white people testifying to white people. White is the default, and brown or black is "other." As much as I may crane my neck to see my own shadow, it drifts behind me, conveniently out of view. As willing as I am to pay attention to hidden racist impulses, they are in the air I breathe.

I unconsciously accept whiteness as the norm, the standard by which all people are judged, and it's a false construct. "Fake," my friend Rev. angel Kyodo Williams, an African American Zen priest and activist known for coining the term "Radical Dharma," calls it. White supremacy is a collective illusion that exists only to secure and maintain power and privilege. And it robs us all of our birthright of belonging to one another, which is the quintessence of feminine wisdom.

Rev. angel has helped me begin the task of recognizing, unpacking, and dismantling my white privilege. Not because my whiteness makes me a bad person, but because white supremacy, even if unintended, makes me less human, and what Rev. angel wants for all people is the full flowering of our humanity. Protesting that I'm the least racist person on the planet or apologizing my head off for accidentally perpetuating institutionalized racism neither contributes to my own awakening nor does people of color any good.

In fact, altruism is a bit of a red herring that can throw us off the track of what matters most: human connection. When good-hearted, politically progressive, spiritually oriented white folks like myself rush in to "fix" the problem of racism and thereby restore justice to those poor, disadvantaged people of color, we are often unconsciously reifying our privilege and further alienating the people we are hoping to "save." This stuff is subtle, it's insidious, and to wake up to it is to defy our cultural conditioning. There is this implicit, irrational threat that if we go against the tide of white privilege we will lose our privilege.

From the corporate boardrooms to the dharma centers of America, we who have white skin collapse into whiteness and forfeit our wholeness. And yet, if we breathe through our defensiveness and become present, taking a clear look at the chains that bind us to what the antiracism scholar Peggy McIntosh calls the "invisible package of unearned assets" that we haul around, we can sever those chains. When we engage in this process in a safe space, as painful as our awakening may initially be, we can, as Rev. angel assures me, "burst into freedom." Thanks to wise women like Rev. angel giving me a loving kick in the ass, my journey of liberation has begun.

Fighting Empire with Love

Christena Cleveland is a renowned millennial social scientist and theologian. She navigates a razor's edge of privilege and marginalization. As an African American woman in a world dominated by white men, Christena challenges those of us who benefit from the structures that give rise to inequality, inviting us to make an effort to recognize and study our privilege, talk about it with other privileged people, and use our power to create space for those who have historically been oppressed to flourish.

Christena also identifies as privileged. Growing up in a highly educated, upwardly mobile African American family, there was little doubt that Christena would graduate from a prestigious college and be successful at whatever she chose to do. Indeed, Christena surpassed expectations, attaining scholarly acclaim from a young age and becoming a professor at a well-regarded university. She has not taken her success for granted—not for a minute. She has planted herself in low-income neighborhoods, living among people who could scarcely imagine a path out of poverty. She has convened groups of girls and given them a place to explore their experiences and dream about other possibilities.

Christena says that a major part of her spiritual path has been "the holiness of perpetual repentance" and that this kind of soul accounting must be a sacred practice for all privileged people. For marginalized people, it is vital to engage in spiritual practices that generate hope and joy—not by numbing their pain or accumulating credentials, but by integrating their suffering with love.

Christena told me about a situation in which her intention to cultivate love yielded startling results. Early in her career, she landed a teaching job at a small, highly conservative Christian college. A small group of young white guys seemed to take boundless pleasure in challenging Christena in the classroom. Genuinely believing that women did not have a divine right to teach men, as their fundamentalist faith had taught them, they asked Christena questions designed to undermine her authority. "I'm smart. I have a PhD in this subject. All of society would have supported me in using my power to lay the smack down," Christena admitted. "But I know you can't fight empire with empire. I decided to try another way." So, alone at home, Christena practiced a meditation based on the Hindu teaching of *namaste*: "The light in me honors the light in you." She translated the Sanskrit phrase into a Judeo-Christian framework she could more easily relate to, visualized her tormentors, and repeated, "The image of God in me greets the image of God in you."

Back in class, whenever one of the boys would raise his hand, Christena would pause, "shoot an imaginary Nerf arrow of love at him," and silently say her prayer before responding: *The image of God in me greets the image of God in you.* In the small space between their rude remarks and Christena's verbal response, the atmosphere relaxed a little. Without any obvious cause, her self-appointed critics soon lost interest in their power game. In fact, toward the end of the semester, Christena invited all her students to a cookie-baking party at her home, and the four guys showed up and, innocent as small children helping their grandmother in the kitchen, appointed themselves her faithful assistants. They helped gather the necessary implements, mix the dough, tend the outdoor fire, and serve up the warm treats. The boys were the last to leave at the end of the evening. Everything shifted after that.

"It's a testament to the power of love," Christena told me. "The point is not to change people's minds or even their behavior. It's not about convincing them that you deserve their respect. When people are sucking the energy out of community they need to feel loved and accepted." One of the young men wrote his final paper on women in ministry and planned to open a conversation about gender reconciliation in his own church. Christena's expression of spiritual generosity, fueled by the fire of her own inner struggle to place love over power, shifted the landscape of the boys' inherited advantage to one of holy tenderness.

"We cannot effect justice without love," Christena says.

Rev. angel Kyodo Williams sings a similar song. "Love and justice are not two," Rev. angel says. "Without inner change, there can be no outer change; without collective change, no change matters."

Only by doing our inner work can we hope to be agents of change in the world. Yet working on ourselves is not enough. Love is the fire that burns down the structures that oppress people and degrade the planet. Justice is the phoenix that rises from those ashes.

HURT PEOPLE HURT PEOPLE

My friend Lyla June Johnston discovered the connective tissue between self-forgiveness and generational healing. Lyla is a youth activist, performance poet, and musician. Part Diné (Navajo), part Cheyenne, and part European American, Lyla carries the possibility of reconciliation imprinted in her DNA. With a degree in environmental anthropology from Stanford University, Lyla uses her education to wake people up to issues of decolonization and help activate the healing of Mother Earth. She has been teaching herself to speak Diné, weaving this indigenous language into her poems, prayers, and songs. She dresses in her Native attire whenever she makes a presentation, claiming her ancestry by calling on her ancestors to be with her as she steps up to the call of these urgent times. Lyla steps up with love.

For most of her life Lyla has identified far more with her Native heritage than her white side. In fact, she often felt ashamed of her Caucasian blood. Until she had an experience while traveling in Europe—the land of the colonizers—that connected her to the spirits of her ancestors there. It was a time of great shattering in Lyla's life. She had literally broken most of her bones jumping out of an upper-story window during an earthquake in Chile and had recently ended a relationship with someone she loved very much. She accepted an invitation to Switzerland to give her body more space to heal and to breathe some perspective back into her life.

One day, as Lyla sat on a rocky outcropping overlooking a valley, she began to sense the presence of her European grandmothers. She felt into their suffering. Tens of thousands of women on that continent had been burned alive as witches, Lyla realized, and maybe even more. These were healers, midwives, wise women. Her Native American community was not the only one to have been brutalized. And this led to another epiphany: genocide does not come out of the blue. It's not like a group of people wake up one day and say, "Let's go murder all the people who have been living on this land we covet and live there ourselves." Something had to have happened to them. "Colonized people colonize people," Lyla says.

This experience of connection with her European ancestors and their story of oppression infused Lyla's broken heart and shifted her perspective. She understood that her Native people had internalized the pain of colonization and needed to actively work on healing themselves so that they would not end up unconsciously perpetuating the cycle of violence.

Lyla initiated the process with her own life. She had grown up around drugs and alcohol, so it had felt natural for her to become a dealer to get through college. She had sold drugs to people she knew couldn't handle them, including women who would be vulnerable to sexual abuse while they were high. Eventually, Lyla found that she had to face the reality of what she had done and open herself to unconditional love from the unseen forces she refers to as "angels," whose presence filled her heart and mind when she surrendered to her own brokenness.

Lyla began to follow the tracks of her behavior back to the wounds of her chaotic childhood, in which substance abuse was rampant and sexual boundaries were sketchy. She realized that she must find forgiveness for herself before she could dedicate her life to the reconciliation of her communities. And so she showed up for the hard labor of inner work, leaning on the love of invisible advocates to give her the strength to face her own demons and opening her heart to everyone she encountered as if they were family. Which we are.

Lyla's subsequent healing—which she attributes entirely to the gifts of the spirits from *all* of her ancestors—has made of her a powerful advocate for restorative justice.

ASK A MUSLIM

Mona Haydar is a Syrian American Muslim, a peacemaker, a poet, and a renowned rapper. The visibility of her hijab (head covering) and her commitment to speaking out on behalf of Muslim women make Mona a constant target for racism, which gives her the ongoing opportunity for forgiveness and reconciliation. She embraces that opportunity.

Mona happens to also be like a daughter to me. In conjunction with a Palestinian Sufi sheik, I (a Jew) coofficiated Mona's marriage to Sebastian, a half-Jewish man, on a remote mountaintop in New Mexico. The marriage is a living symbol of the reconciliation between the children of Abraham (and Sarah and Hagar), of a Muslim and a Jew, of a woman of color and a white man. Sebastian converted to Islam, without ever rejecting his Jewish roots. When Mona was in labor with their first child, I stayed up all night stuffing grape leaves with her Syrian mother. As the sun rose the next morning, I sat quietly while Mona's husband and his mother-in-law unrolled their prayer rugs and, kneeling together, greeted the day with salat (prayer).

I watched with awe (and a degree of pride, I cannot deny) as Mona rose to fame for her "Ask a Muslim" mission. Shortly after their son was born, Sebastian and Mona moved to the East Coast to be closer to their families. In the middle of a New England winter, the couple set up a table outside the Cambridge Public Library, offering donuts and coffee and inviting passersby to engage in conversation with actual Muslims, individuals who happen to represent a deeply misunderstood branch of the human family right now. People could ask anything from "Is your religion oppressive to women?" to "What do you think about the Boston Red Sox winning the World Series?" The couple addressed each question with patience, intelligence, and good cheer.

Then, in the midst of working on her graduate degree at Union Theological Seminary (a traditionally Christian institution), with a toddler at home and another baby on the way, Mona managed to write and produce an award-winning music video that celebrates a woman's right to "wrap her hijab" as a symbol of her love for the One. She went on to produce a series of songs and videos that have garnered great acclaim and helped wake up the world to the poison of sexism and the beauty of Islam.

It is love that characterizes Mona's activism. It is not fancy academic jargon. It is not jingoism. It isn't even self-righteous diatribes against Islamophobia. It is *rahman* (mercy) and *rahim* (compassion). It is a resounding eloquence, a sweet tenderness, and a mischievous sense of humor. Mona is habitually other focused, yet she speaks fearlessly about institutionalized misogyny, calling on men to treat women as the doorway to the Divine. "Paradise," said the Prophet Muhammad, "lies at the feet of the Mother." Mona is first and foremost a Muslim. Her love for all beings overflows from the vessel of her relationship with Allah.

deepening

> Write a letter of forgiveness to someone who has hurt you or given you cause to despair for the future of the planet and all who dwell here. You do not (necessarily) need to send it. Share it with someone you trust, asking them to bear loving witness without giving you advice.

You may also choose to burn it in a ritual fire or cast it into a moving body of water. Consider the possibility that in the ritual act of forgiving you are cutting karmic ties that bind you, clearing the way for your own liberation and the liberation of all beings with whom you come into contact.

Teach me how to grieve
The night spills over with stars
Teach me how to die

DYING

The Ultimate Spiritual Practice

opening

Her body is disappearing, though her heart still beats, her breath still puffs a little in, a little out, her eyes are luminous, and she's still making jokes. Jokes about dying, mostly. Being with her now is like trekking on a beautiful new planet where she is an honored elder and you are a visitor. This is the most hallowed space you have ever encountered. Someone you love is leaving her life behind. What's left of her is twisted with pain. And there is nowhere else you would rather be. The rapture of the moment is thick enough to seal all the cracks in your own life. She is, with her quiet dying, bestowing an explosion of blessings.

Then there is the baby who was born and died at the same time. Now the mother's face has aged from 25 to 105 as she presses it against the perfect face of her dead baby boy and soundlessly howls. You stand by like an oak tree in the middle of the pediatric intensive care unit, providing shade from the glaring radiance of tragedy.

And your piano teacher. He leaves a letter, explaining that he could no longer bear the pain, that he tried, tried hard, but that the bridge beckoned like a long-sought lover. He blows kisses in the form of special messages to the closest people in his mighty little circle of support. You never gave up on him, and he is grateful. But he is done. You try not to imagine his thoughts as he tumbled through the sky and into the river below. You focus on the peace he left behind.

You remember the time your older sister's first child was born, how you shared a hospital gown with your younger sister—she had her left arm in one side and you had your right in the other—and in three big pushes the most beautiful creature you could imagine washed from the ocean of your sister's body onto the shore of this world and nothing, nothing, would ever be the same. The deathbed now feels like the birth bed felt then. Like the universe is taking in a big inhale, recalibrating, and exhaling a new reality. Like God enters through a fissure that opens only on occasions like these, and you know you'd better pay attention, or you might miss her appearance.

The air around your dying friend is charged in the same way. Your culture tells you something terrible is happening here. Something tragic. In some ways this is true. A being that has filled the horizon of your days is diminishing like a comet across the night sky and soon will consist of only memory molecules and maybe the occasional messages from the other side. For now, that is okay with you. For now, you are showing up for this gift, this rattling breath, this hand like a sparrow's wing nestled in yours. The sound of your own voice as you sing a Native prayer you learned when you were a small girl and have not thought of since. Till now. Now when you are entering the temple of your beloved's holy dying and kneeling there.

You know your own death is coming, sooner than it once seemed. You glimpse its approach in the deepening lines around your mouth and eyes, how it takes a while after you get up in the morning for your back to stop hurting. You can feel your grip loosening on your ambitions, orgasms are no longer the main goal of lovemaking, and it's easier to sit beside a pond and do nothing but follow the trajectory of a dragonfly's journey with your eyes.

Aging is no longer the enemy you fear and disdain because of what lies at the end of it. Instead, it is a horse you have mounted that walks—does not gallop—into vast new stretches of the human experience. You are entering the wilderness. You are not afraid.

Bearing Witness

It amazes me when full-grown adults tell me they have never experienced the death of anyone close to them other than elderly grandparents. So far, I have had an incarnation rife with dying: my big brother to cancer when I was seven and he was ten; my first boyfriend in a gun accident when we were teenagers; my father when I was barely thirty and he just over sixty—younger than my husband is now—and dozens of close friends and fond acquaintances. But the most shattering loss of all was of my daughter Jenny when she was fourteen. Jenny's death was a tsunami that rearranged the entire landscape of my life. She is the reason I am writing this book, the reason you are reading it.

My friend Ondrea Levine, whom we met in chapter 10, sits with the dying, listening with love as they unburden their hearts and let go of their lives. "I am the Death Ma," Ondrea says about herself, with a good-natured shrug. "I always have been. This is what I came here for."

I can relate. After my daughter's death I became a grief counselor, because the only thing that helped me make sense of what had happened to me was to show up for others as they showed up for the immensity of what had happened to them. Pretty soon my community began asking me to sit with the dying as well as the bereaved. Eventually I accepted invitations to officiate a couple of memorial services, and that has now grown to dozens. Each time I sit with someone whose heart has been shattered, or bear witness to someone as they take leave of this world, or gather my community to celebrate the life of a loved one, I have a sense of being lined up with my own inner architecture. There's a geometric resonance. It feels like a homecoming.

We don't all have to have signed such a cosmic contract as Ondrea and I seem to have done in order to experience the holiness of death and dying and the transformational power of grief and grieving. But we can cultivate our intimacy with these sacred spaces. It takes some effort and courage to consciously break through the veil that Western society has spun around death. We are conditioned to see death as a failure rather than as a pilgrimage.

Once we have made our way to the bedside of one dying beloved, however, it gets easier to gain access to the next. Pretty soon, we will find ourselves at ease facing the mystery of the body dissolving back into its source. Because of our experience being with the dying, people around us take comfort when we walk through the door. Our fearlessness reassures the terrified, who may be casting about for some ground to stand on when the whole world seems to be dissolving beneath their feet. Dying is rarely a tidy and predictable process. We need each other.

Yet, no matter how many bedsides I sit at, I still find myself getting thrown off-balance sometimes by the kerfuffle that arises around the death of a loved one. Those of us who are giving care can get triggered, and our own unresolved wounds rise to the surface like gray foam in a pot of simmering black beans. Friends and family members inadvertently, yet inevitably, step on one another's (psychic) toes. Ordinarily mild-mannered people might suddenly take charge and boss everyone else around, seemingly oblivious to the impact on those closest to the dying. Others may bite their tongues and seethe, feeling disenfranchised and misunderstood. Meanwhile, the person who is leaving this world gets on with the most momentous task of her life.

The invitation here is to be kind to ourselves and one another as we step up to hold the dying and the bereaved. This means remembering that the mystery of death is likely to serve as a catalyst for our insecurities and self-doubts. But it is also a portal for some of the most potent and transformational experiences we can have as human beings. Mindfulness practice is our friend in the land of death. All we need to do is watch our fear and pain arise, name it, smile and wave, maybe even take it into our arms for a moment and cradle it until it relaxes, and then return our attention to the wild mercy of what is real.

When we come to the house of the dying and bear loving witness to the person whose turn it is to lie in bed there, we are doing all that needs to be done. There's nothing to fix, because nothing is broken. We are not required to come up with any explanations, because the only useful response to the mystery of death is awe and wonderment. We may bring tea, wipe the dying one's forehead with a cool washcloth, empty the puke bucket, read some poetry aloud, or reshuffle the iTunes playlist, but the most important thing is to sit quietly and bear witness. Bear loving witness.

I'll Be Demeter, and You Be Persephone

Every bereaved mother I know identifies with the Greek mythic mother Demeter, goddess of the harvest, whose daughter Persephone is abducted by Hades, king of the underworld. Fucking Hades. He abducted my daughter, too. Except that, unlike Demeter, I failed to negotiate a treaty to get her back. Like Demeter, however, I tried. The gods know I did. I even managed to travel to the underworld, rowing my lonely boat across the waters of death, calling her name. But my voice only bounced off the dark walls and echoed in my own skull: *Jenny, Jenny, Jenny* . . . Defeated, I headed home without her.

Truly, when a child dies, the crops fail. What we may previously have taken for granted—abundant harvest of grain, profusion of flowers, sparrow song, and sunlight on the water—withers. The world becomes barren, and its inhabitants starve. When Jenny died, winter fell over my inner landscape. It was during this time of grief and spiritual poverty that my heart was imperceptibly reconfigured and my soul invisibly transformed. This alchemy could not have occurred had I not taken the journey of descent. I had no choice but to go down. To go all the way down. I am a mother whose child was taken by the Lord of Death. Fourteen years old, on the verge of womanhood, Jenny crashed my car (the chariot of Hades!) and disappeared (into a chasm in the earth!).

In the Greek myth, Demeter is the fertility goddess, and Persephone is her blossoming daughter, whom she adores with every fiber of her mother heart. One day, as Persephone is picking flowers in a quiet field, Hades bursts through a crack in the ground and whisks her away. As the earth is swallowing her, Persephone cries out, and her mother catches the heart-wrenching end of her lamentation. Splintered by grief and rage, inconsolable, Demeter neglects her divine tasks and the earth, once fertile, grows desolate. The people are hungry, and the gods are mortified. They beg Demeter to get over herself, let her daughter go, and get back to work creating plenitude. Demeter does not cease from mourning. She cannot. Nor should she.

Finally Zeus strikes a deal with Hades to return Persephone to life. Hades agrees, but first he tricks Persephone into eating a few pomegranate seeds. It is well known that those of us who eat of the fruit of the underworld will never be free of the grasp of the underworld. So Persephone is allowed to ascend back to the land of life, where she is reunited with her beloved mother, but only for half the year. The other half of the year she has to return to the land of death and rule there as consort to Hades.

What I wouldn't give to be offered such an arrangement.

THE KATES

I have two friends named Kate who lost their daughters. Both Kates are Demeters. They raged against their losses, refused to nourish life, and made the dangerous descent into the land of death in search of their abducted daughters. One Kate is the mother of Nina, a talented composer and world traveler who was murdered at age twenty-nine while taking a walk during her sister's destination wedding in the Caribbean. The other Kate is the mother of Anna-Mirabai, who, like my Jenny, was fourteen and flowering when she was struck by an impaired driver while riding her bicycle home from her job at her mom's yoga studio on the first day of summer vacation.

I will never forget the moments I received word of these two tragedies. Having somehow managed to bear the unbearable myself, I knew it would be touch-and-go for my friends. They might or might not survive the plunge into hell. All I could do, as a sister-mother in the club no one wants to belong to, was commit to standing beside them. Even as a Demeter myself, I knew I could not console these goddesses. Instead, I was bound to make mistakes, say the wrong things, impose my own experience on the glaringly blank screen of their shattered hearts. I would babble when I should be quiet, and I would forget to call when they most needed me to reach out because they were incapable of initiating a plea for help. But my ineptitude did not make any difference. Nor did my expertise as a Demeter. The Kates had to navigate their own landscapes of loss. What mattered was that I said yes. I did not turn from their suffering. I bore witness. This is our task as women on the path of transformational love. We guard one another's hearts with our lives.

Persephone ascends in her own way, I suppose. She returns as a passion for justice, a project that serves the community, an artistic endeavor. We catch her fragrance in the melting snow of March and see her face poking through the warming garden in the first purple crocus. We hear her voice in the kids who grow up in our midst and set off on their life path and come home with children of their own in their arms. Her wisdom resounds in our life-affirming choices, in our fierce compassion for the brokenhearted, in our willingness to abide in unknowing.

SKY DANCING

Lama Tsultrim Allione is part of a luminous wave emerging from the ocean of feminine mysticism. Steeped in the legacy of the renowned Tantric yogini Machig Labdrön in the Tibetan Buddhist tradition, Lama Tsultrim embodies the wild wisdom of the *dakini*, the "sky dancers." These feminine energies appear in our lives and stir up our complacent practices, awaken our slumbering consciousness, and cut through our attachments. A dakini helps us dissolve the ego and fully engage with reality as it is. Dakini energy is a synthesis of nitty-gritty embodiment and vast openness, of passionate engagement and equanimity.

Like me, and maybe you, Lama Tsultrim stepped foot on the spiritual path at a young age. When she was only nineteen her quest led her to India and Tibet, where she encountered the wisdom that would sweep the rest of her life into its arms. Known for her teachings on Chöd—an intensive practice with its roots in Tibetan shamanism and Mahayana Buddhism during which practitioners willingly "feed" their bodies to various "guests," including their "demons," as a way to develop profound generosity and cut through ego clinging—Lama Tsultrim has worked with thousands of seekers to help them enter the heart of their deepest fears and transform these fears into allies. The demons are not external; rather, they are the very issues in our lives that drain us, such as depression, anxiety, and addiction. Lama Tsultrim has practiced and taught her way through loss upon loss of her own. In fact, it was the death of Tsultrim's third child from sudden infant death syndrome (SIDS) that drove her search for an embodied feminine wisdom from her own tradition.

One of the first (and youngest) Western woman to take monastic vows in Nepal, Lama Tsultrim came to grips with a fierce longing to practice the dharma as a householder, and she went home to the West in her midtwenties to start a family. Following her daughter's death, Tsultrim returned to Nepal, where she found the biography of Machig Labdrön, a unique Tibetan female teacher from the eleventh century and the founder of the ancient Vajrayana practice of Chöd. Following Machig's lead, she received transmission in Chöd and eventually began to teach it, developing the method she calls "Feeding Your Demons."

Finding what was hers to do and be in this lifetime did not magically rescue Lama Tsultrim from participation in the human condition. In 2010, her beloved husband of twenty-two years, David, unexpectedly died in his sleep. This is what I wanted to know about during a recent conversation with her: What was it like for her as a lifelong spiritual practitioner and teacher to lose her life companion, her devoted dharma brother, her lover?

David died suddenly at the age of fifty-four, having shown not a sign of physical distress prior to his heart attack. He was a former dancer, robust and vigorous, who oversaw the building of many of the structures on the grounds of Tara Mandala, the Buddhist community Lama Tsultrim founded and guides in

Colorado, and who tended to the many tasks of mountain life, often on horseback. He was also a dedicated practitioner in his own right and prior to his death had attained rarefied states of awakening. Three days before he died, Dave had said enigmatically to his wife, "I feel like my body is dissolving."

The night Dave died, Tsultrim was sleeping alone in the temple a few miles away from their home, as she sometimes did when she was working intensively on a project. She did not hear from him the following morning, which was unusual because they always checked in with each other when they were apart. Tsultrim asked her assistant, Sarah, to go to the house to check on him, thinking that maybe he was out on his horse or had gone somewhere and forgotten his phone. Sarah delayed going because she intuited something was wrong. When she did finally go, she found David face down in bed, cold and unresponsive. She raced back to the temple to tell Lama Tsultrim, who jumped in her car.

As she made her way from the temple to the house, Tsultrim was vividly aware that the five-minute drive was taking her to a place she had never been, that this familiar landscape would be transformed by what she was about to face, that life as she knew it was over. When she found David in bed, she immediately realized he was gone: blood had already pooled at the base of his body, and rigor mortis was setting in. She leaned over and kissed his cold arm, thinking, *I will never kiss this body again.*

This is the love of a woman for her man. This is the love of an esteemed teacher for her earthly husband. Spiritual awakening does not leave us immune to the human condition. Quite the opposite. It brings us into the heart of reality, where we mourn and rage, bow and give thanks, ache and surrender. Ever a sky dancer, Tsultrim allowed her heart to dissolve into the vast sky of grief.

In the midst of her anguish, Tsultrim turned toward the pain. Finding herself face to face with samsara (the cycle of death and rebirth that characterizes the suffering of the human condition), the lama realized she could honor her lifelong vow to liberate all sentient beings by practicing *tonglen* ("sending and taking"), breathing in the suffering of all beings everywhere who were grieving the death of a beloved and through the out breath sending them back peace and comfort. It is a Tibetan practice beautifully articulated by Pema Chödrön and one I have often used myself in times of overwhelming feelings of pain or confusion.

"At first I didn't think I could take any more sadness," Tsultrim said. "It was already unbearable. I felt like I was in a pressure cooker. But the results of the practice were paradoxical and surprising. I experienced a relief from my own grief by opening to the pain of others. Through this my heart had to expand beyond my personal constricted grief to embrace their suffering." Lama Tsultrim's participation in the mystery of grief became yet another doorway through the truth of suffering to the truth of interbeing.

▼

Dipa Ma (1911–1989), a Vipassana Buddhist master from Southeast Asia, is another woman who chose family life as a path of awakening, and with this choice came excruciating loss. In the space of a few years, Dipa Ma lost two small children and her beloved husband and then grew seriously ill herself. Pretty much paralyzed by grief, she realized that if she did not get out of bed and begin practicing meditation, she would die. Dipa Ma did not engage in contemplative practice as a means for curing or transcending suffering. Rather, she developed great skill in cultivating mindfulness in every circumstance, becoming fully present to whatever she was experiencing—no matter how painful—and resting in it.

So adept was Dipa Ma at engaging everyday life as a monastic opportunity that her teachings became especially relevant to householders. Dipa Ma guided nursing mothers to be fully present as they nursed and busy accountants to do their calculations mindfully. She taught with love and humor and also uncompromising rigor. Dipa Ma was the quiet energy behind the wave of the American mindfulness movement. The contemporary American Vipassana (insight meditation) masters Sharon Salzberg, Jack Kornfield, and Joseph Goldstein consider her to have been one of their most powerful and beloved influences.

The Holy Land of Mourning

Grief is an individual journey, and there are no rules to follow nor laws you can break. It takes as long as it takes (forever, in my case, and maybe in yours, too), so there's no point in judging yourself or others for not "getting over it" swiftly enough.

People will often avoid mentioning our loved one's name for fear it will remind us and make us sad. As if we could ever forget! As if we had stopped for a moment being sad! Our sorrow is directly connected to our love, and we refuse to be shamed into relinquishing it. In fact, when someone is brave enough to speak of our loved one, it can be such a relief. It means she existed; she mattered. For a moment there is another being to help lift and carry the great weight of her memory, bringing her back from the private shadows of our own heart into the generous light of community.

When someone close to us dies, we get to be creative about how we honor them. We don't have to follow the funerary practices of mainstream society. We can mourn our loved ones according to our inner directives. We may pray in an array of sacred languages or skip religiosity altogether and go straight for poetry and the blues. If we are not wedded to a particular spiritual tradition, we might draw from them all, weaving a tapestry of ritual to warm and sustain us when our soul has been flung across the universe and we fear we will never find our way home.

My friend Elaine, a Jewish Sufi Buddhist, practiced for her death. She even held a dress rehearsal for her burial. I was there. She had decided she wanted to be buried in an eco-friendly manner, and so we did some research and settled on a hand-woven willow basket casket, designed to cradle her shrouded body and melt back into the earth and nourish the high desert soil of Lama Mountain in New Mexico, where she chose to be laid to rest.

As her death approached, Elaine's children and grandchildren gathered from all over the country at her home in Taos. It was an unseasonably warm November day, the sky washed in that rarefied shade of periwinkle that has drawn artists to New Mexico forever. We unboxed the casket, set it in the garden, and helped Elaine climb in. Then we each grabbed a handle and lifted her. We strode around the yard, bursting into an off-key rendition of "Swing Low, Sweet Chariot" while Elaine made fun of herself and us. When we placed the basket back on the ground, Elaine grew serious and summoned us.

"I would like each of you to kneel beside me and tell me what you most want me to hear," she directed. "Why should you wait for my funeral to say nice things?" So we did, her daughters, her grandsons, her closest friends. One by one, we reached into her basket casket, awkwardly encircled Elaine's frail collarbones, and whispered in her ear what we loved best about her, what of her we would carry inside us when she was gone.

We had time to do Elaine's death the way we wanted, as a community, and the way she wanted. Elaine died as she had lived—bathed in beauty, blessed by wonderment. When my daughter was killed in the accident years earlier, I had no chance to prepare and no hope of saying good-bye. Thrown to my knees in shock, I nevertheless intuited that I had to take charge of what happened to my child's body or I would regret it later. With the support of my mother and my sister, my older daughter and my partner, I made the decision to bring Jenny's body home so that everyone who loved her could come say good-bye. Having little prior experience to guide us, we made it all up as we went along. I write about this experience in more detail in my memoir, *Caravan of No Despair*. I wish everyone knew that they have the right and the power to take up the task of honoring their loved ones in their own way, as we did.

A group of women gathered at the funeral home to wash my daughter's broken body, sing to her and pray for her, and anoint her with fragrant oils. Then they wrapped her in her favorite blue dolphin sarong, leaving her face exposed so we could kiss it. We loaded her into the back of our pickup truck and drove her across town to the house where only the day before she had woken in her own bed, alive. One friend built an open casket from red cedar, and another brought over an antique wooden platform on which we laid Jenny's body in front of the living room window, which opened out toward the sea of mesa land to the west.

All day and through the night our community gathered, filling Jenny's open casket with flowers and sacred objects, surrounding her with juniper and piñon boughs, sprigs of wild sage and long-stemmed roses. Drawing on all the world's wisdom ways, we chanted the Hebrew *kaddish*, Sufi *dhikr*, and Hindu *kirtan*; we sang African American spirituals and Native American hymns in praise of the Earth. My friend Father Bill blessed her body and commended her to the light, invoking Quan Yin and Mother Mary. Buddhist practitioners sat in silence or intoned *Om mani padme hum*. The teenagers wailed over their friend's body and then disappeared into her room to do whatever teenagers do to grieve their dead. The collective intelligence of the community, as it turned out, fueled by the electric fire of a mother's anguish, knew exactly what to do. We mourned Jenny in a fully feminine way, without a plan, responsive to the wild wisdom of the moment.

At one point, one of the mothers who had brought her daughter over to pay her respects looked around the house in dismay at the crowd of people praying in multiple languages, nibbling and chatting at the kitchen counter, even laughing and gossiping in small clusters, and she grabbed her daughter's hand.

"Let's get out of here," she said. "These people are energy vampires."

Even in my shattered state, I understood what she was trying to say. She felt that the people who had gathered in our home were somehow getting off on the energy of tragedy, that it gave them a sense of self-importance to be part of it. But my own experience was that my community had rushed in to hold me up when I couldn't hold myself. Every one of their prayers was a buoy I could rest on in the perilous ocean of my despair. This woman's words made me question that I was doing it all wrong. That I was failing to mourn my child correctly.

Listen, friends: there is no wrong way to grieve. I know that now. There's no right way, either. In the wake of Jenny's accident I was too broken, too vulnerable to withstand harsh judgment. No one had provided me with a map I could follow through the wilderness to which I had been so suddenly exiled. I was flailing, doing my best to honor my child at the same time that I could scarcely remember how to breathe. But I persevered, drawing on every sacred teaching from every spiritual tradition I had ever encountered. I was determined to shower Jenny's journey with blessings and was grateful for every friend and neighbor who showed up to blunder along beside me in this horrendous and sacred mystery.

Dancing with the Dead

In Mexico, where I have spent much of my life, death is not treated as the heavy, almost shameful event that it is in the United States and other contemporary Euro-Western cultures. Día de los Muertos (Day of the Dead), a fusion of ancient Mesoamerican religious rituals and Roman Catholicism, is a perfect example of befriending death.

Before the Spanish Conquest, the Aztec people celebrated the ancestors in the summer, dedicating their rituals to the goddess Mictecacihuatl, Lady of the Dead. When the colonizers introduced Christian culture to what is now Mexico, these ancient practices morphed, flowed into the liturgical calendar, and blended with All Saints' Day and All Souls' Day. In this hybrid mestizo tradition, November 1 is dedicated to children who have died and is known as Día de los Angelitos (Little Angels' Day), and November 2 is set aside to pay homage to all the other departed loved ones.

In light of crucial concerns about cultural appropriation of indigenous traditions by well-meaning white folks, I recommend engaging this potent ritual with extra care and respect if it is not already part of your ancestral path. For Anglo-Americans who choose to walk through these gates with our eyes open and our hearts humble, the Day of the Dead can cover a lot of spiritual ground. It honors the ancestors, it supports the souls of our loved ones on their journey through the land of death to whatever sublime space we hope they will abide in, and it normalizes death as a natural part of the life cycle.

In many regions of Latin America and the American Southwest, traditional festivities veer away from the grim and into the playful. Children decorate sugar skulls. Families set up altars with photos, quirky things the deceased enjoyed in life, like a lucky baseball card or a travel mug, peanut butter or beer. They ring bells and gongs and leave trails of marigolds so the dead can find their way from the other world to this one and back again.

The ceremony serves to integrate our losses into the cells of our bodies and helps reweave the fabric of community. It acknowledges the full spectrum of our experience of death from pain to tenderness to hushed awe to wild liberation.

Where Día de los Muertos lightens the heart of the bereaved, certain traditions from other cultures can help us make our way across the threshold of death. *The Tibetan Book of the Dead*, for instance, is an ancient sacred text meant to be whispered in the ear of the person who is dying and read aloud afterward. It encourages the dying person to recognize all the difficult or frightening images, thoughts, and emotions that may arise during the death process as projections of the dying person's own mind and not ultimately true. This text is designed to equip the person with the clarity and energy they need to move unimpeded through the *bardos* (transitional realms between life, death, and rebirth) and straight to the light. While the practice is most potent in the first seventy-two hours following death, it is continued in modified form for a full forty-nine days.

In Judaism, the practice of sitting *shiva* assists those closest to the deceased to fully focus on mourning their loved one and in doing so to metabolize the trauma of loss. Mourners sit on cushions on the floor for the first seven days following a significant loss, as a physical reflection of being brought low by grief. Symbolic of being torn apart by loss, we rend a garment that we wear throughout that week. We drape the mirrors with cloth so that our attention is turned from outward appearances to the inner realms of contemplation.

Community members gather to offer their condolences and join in the daily chanting of the kaddish (the Jewish mourners' prayer). They bring food for the family so that the people closest to the deceased do not have to be distracted by worldly responsibilities and instead may give themselves over to the experience of meeting a world that no longer has their beloved father or mother, husband or child in it. This ritual helps the bereaved actualize the customary phrase uttered to those who mourn: "May their memory be a blessing."

Whenever we engage spiritual practices from cultures other than our own, it is wise to do so mindfully and respectfully so that we don't careen over the line of universal love into the territory of cultural appropriation. Still, I believe that the world's great wisdom traditions offer nourishment for all beings and that when we partake of them with care and gratitude, we sustain ourselves and become a source of nurturance for the world. When someone we love dies, we need all the help we can get to survive the trauma and enter the land of the sacred.

Messages from the Other Side

Opening our hearts and minds to the presence of our loved ones who have died, we may find them everywhere: in the way the light washes across the eastern mountain slopes as the sun is setting in the west and reminds us of the rapture of our best friend's face as he assented to the voyage of dying; in the sound of a grandchild's laughter, so much like our sister's, her Great-Aunt Rosario; in the arrival of a flock of sparrows on the lawn just as we were missing our husband so intensely we couldn't breathe.

I once believed that contact with deceased loved ones had to have certain features to qualify as bona fide visitations. Visions, voices, clear dreams with pointed messages, fond farewells. But intimacy with death has widened the margins for me, and now I feel the presence of my loved ones in a vast galaxy of spaces. When Elaine died I expected to have dreams, to feel her sitting beside me in the morning as I sipped my coffee just the way she liked it from the purple pottery cup her daughter took from the dishwasher and handed to me the day after her death.

But nothing happened. "How could someone so alive be so gone?" Ganga Das lamented. The landscape of our lives had been filled with Elaine, and now neither of us could access her. Then, months later, as we hiked a trail we had walked dozens of times with Elaine over the years, Ganga Das looked over to a tangle of sagebrush and said, "Huh. Someone must have found an earring." I had already passed the spot, but something compelled me to turn back and take a look. Yup. Dangling in the center of the cluster, at eye level, was *my* earring. Elaine had once made a pair for me, and they were my favorites. She had had a successful jewelry business for many years, called Gypsy Moon, for which she designed elaborate art pieces from glass beads and semiprecious stones. Right after her death I had lost one of the earrings and had been heartbroken that I couldn't go to my friend for a replacement. This may have been the only pair like it that Elaine ever made, softly shaded in browns and grays—uncharacteristic hues for Elaine, who wore mostly bright purple and turquoise and would invariably quip, when I showed up wearing earth tones, "What, that's a color?" I shrieked with joy and scooped Ganga Das into a hug. Our friend had dropped a little love bomb in our midst.

▼

A couple of weeks before she left this world, Loretta Ortiz y Pino, a revered pediatrician in our community, said to me, "Hey, Mirabai, how about I come visit you when I die?" I was sitting at her bedside. Loretta had end-stage ovarian cancer. Her voice was bright, like a child who had just had a great idea.

Loretta had a secret talent: she received visits from the souls of people who died. The primary message in every one of these encounters was love. Each visit emphasized the importance of living lives of gratitude and reaching out to everyone—strangers and those closest to us—with kindness.

"I'd like that," I said. "I'll try to be open enough to recognize you."

That same day, Loretta asked her spouse, Melissa, to fetch something from the closet. Melissa smiled knowingly and emerged with a jean jacket that one of Loretta's favorite nieces had embellished for her several years ago. An image of Our Lady of Guadalupe, made of green, red, and yellow sequins, covered the back. There was a Wonder Woman patch on one breast pocket and a Smokey Bear patch on the other. Starting at the base of one sleeve and snaking around the back of the neck and down the other sleeve was embroidered my favorite Beatles lyric of all time, proclaiming that the love we take in the end is equal to the love we make throughout. I had just posted that quote on my Facebook page days earlier.

When Loretta died, I began wearing the jacket in her memory. The day before her memorial service (which I had the honor of officiating), I had the jacket on while I was out grocery shopping. Not one, not even half a dozen, but more than twenty people, mostly strangers, commented on it. They didn't just say, "Cool jacket" and walk on by. They stopped, they touched me, they turned me around. One young woman even waited for me outside the store because a couple had walked out talking about the jacket and she wanted to see it for herself.

"Can I take a picture?" she asked, and I nodded. Afterward she hugged me as if I had mended something broken in her soul.

There was no doubt: Loretta was with me. I saw it in the wide-open expressions on each face. There was not a stranger among them, though I had never met them before. They radiated unconditional love, just like Loretta had. It was a little channel of Loretta love that opened up in the midst of the marketplace.

Turning Your Heart Outward

Where death touches our lives, it transfigures the inner landscape. Nothing will ever be the same after someone we love has left this world. Whether they drew their last breath at one hundred or never had a chance to draw their first breath at birth, our loved ones who have died seem to teach us the most about being alive. And yet our consumerist culture is so busy promoting vapid entertainment that most of us have little practice in turning our attention toward our suffering and resting in the darkness where the treasures lie.

Selah. This is the mysterious word used again and again in the Psalms to signify a sacred pause, a breath in the flow of prayer that allows us to sink into the wisdom it imparts. *Selah.* Stop and listen. "I call out to the Lord and he answers me from his holy mountain. Selah." (Psalms 3:4).

My friend and colleague Joanne Cacciatore—known to the many bereaved beings whose broken hearts she tends as "Dr. Jo"—understands the power of pausing to linger in the sacred territory of grief. A specialist in traumatic bereavement, Dr. Jo is also a Zen practitioner who advocates for "green" mental health to care for those suffering traumatic grief, teaching a variety of mindfulness techniques and engaging the gifts of the natural world to help navigate the mystery of heartbreak. Although I met Dr. Jo when I presented at one of her conferences for families of children who have died, she ended up ministering to my own broken heart, which years after my daughter's death still throbs with sorrow. Dr. Jo gets that it always will and that this pain is sacred. She too is a bereaved mother who has given herself over to bearing loving witness to hundreds of other bereaved families.

What Dr. Jo has discovered by companioning people in their darkest descent is that human beings have a deep need to be present with our losses rather than turn away from them. Having a circle of support in this process is invaluable. When we feel held in the reality of our pain, we are gradually able to turn our hearts outward and embrace the pain of others.

Dr. Jo has created a "carefarm" on the outskirts of Sedona, Arizona, which she has named Selah House in honor of the deep soul breath this space offers. At Selah House, the traumatically bereaved can take refuge and be with their experience without anyone trying to medicate them or otherwise banish them from the tender and transformational terrain of their shattered hearts. Dr. Jo has gathered a family of animals at the carefarm, all of whom have suffered abuse or neglect. When mourners come to the farm, they find solace and connection among these rescued creatures. They feed them and groom them, take them on walks or sit and cry beside them.

"When we see the suffering of others, we feel connected to a matrix that is both terrifying and reassuring," Dr. Jo says. This is when hearts soften and turn outward. If we follow the impulse to be of use to other beings in pain, our own pain can become redemptive. "Once you begin to feel better, don't leave. Stay to help another." By caring for rescue animals we can come home to our place in the web of all life.

A powerful exemplar of the feminine mystic, Dr. Jo builds a bridge between responding with compassion to the suffering of others and creating peace on Earth. "We can't rush to meaning," she says. "We need to stay in the middle of the fire, the center of our pain, long enough for it to transform. This is alchemy. This is where fierce compassion is born." From this place of transmuted pain we cannot help but act as a force of love and healing in the world. It begins with saying yes to the terrible blessing of death.

AND SO

From the ancient Maya to Vajrayana Buddhism, from Celtic Christianity to Greek mythology, many of the world's great spiritual traditions suggest that when we die we must navigate the challenges of a liminal terrain on our way to everlasting peace. This strikes me as a masculine paradigm, rooted in a martial model. It depicts the soul as a warrior of light in battle against the forces of darkness. If the deceased prevails, he earns a ticket to a heavenly abode. If he fails, he is consigned to a realm of suffering, or at he the least becomes lost in illusion.

The way of the feminine is to soften into the arms of the unknown. Death is the ultimate mystery, charged with awe, weighted by trepidation, redeemed by promises of deep rest and true seeing. All we really know is that we do not know. And knowing is not required. Striking deals with gods is not required. What we can do is meet *what is* with tenderness and curiosity.

This may mean welcoming suffering—either our own or the pain of a dying loved one—and opening wider and wider to the truth of impermanence and the primacy of love. As the body of the mother unfastens to deliver the new human into the waiting world, so our bodies come undone as we release our souls into the mystery that my friend Ram Dass names "Soul Land." In Spanish, giving birth is called *dar a luz*, "to give to light." Dying is offering the light back to the Divine. Jewish wisdom teachings suggest that when we yield to the holy mystery of dying, it becomes as gentle as removing a hair from a cup of milk.

Anyone who has had the privilege of being with someone as they died (or just afterward) knows how transformational it can be to bear witness to such a primal and exalted moment. It's easy to forget that our own dying can be an opportunity for awakening. If we accept that we are more than the body, then that which remains beyond the physical form is embarking on the most momentous spiritual adventure of all. By showing up for the voyage with our hearts open and our consciousness tethered to liberation, our death can become what the Sufis call our "wedding night with the Beloved." A homecoming. A celebration.

May we return in joy.

deepening

Write two letters: one from yourself to a loved one who has died, sharing everything you may have left unsaid, and the other to yourself from a loved one who has died, with everything you long to hear. (For help getting started, see "Writing Practice Guidelines" on page 223.)

Her Presence: a light
Her teachings: refuge
Her family: your own

TAKING REFUGE

Teachers, Teachings, and Soul Family

opening

You follow the footprints of the Beloved across
manifold spiritual landscapes. You catch the same
ancient, spicy aroma of love in Judaism that you have
tasted in Islam. Your attraction to the lush sensuality
of Hinduism does not in any way preclude the
way you rest in the intellectual purity of Buddhism.
Contemplating the Tao Te Ching strengthens what the
Hopi elders have taught you: that the Earth is alive,
that she is your Mother, that she is the love of your life.

Institutionalized religious authorities discourage this
kind of roaming; they will call you a lost soul. You lie
down with the Beloved in so many forms, the purists
will call you a slut. The more open-minded may still
accuse you of hoping to get to water by digging many
shallow wells. As if you were a fool. You are no fool.
You are in love, and you will use every available means
to reach the living waters of love itself, which you can't
help but notice bubbling up from the altar of every
sacred space you have ever entered, including—and
maybe especially—the wild spaces of this earth.

You embrace your Beloved through your friendship with Jesus alone or through Jesus plus Buddha. You walk one path or three or eleven different spiritual paths that all bring you home to the One Love. Maybe you say, "No, thank you" to any kind of organized religion and, instead, cultivate a direct relationship with the Beloved in the temple of your own heart. The singular true believers will advise you against all of this multiplicity, recommending that you pick a single tradition and "go deep." As if your polyamorous spiritual proclivities render you a dilettante. They will mistakenly judge your way as superficial and undisciplined, rather than as the mind-blowingly, heart-openingly, soul-transfiguringly rigorous spiritual practice that it is.

You don't care that much what they think anyway. You are not about to miss any opportunity to encounter your Beloved and bow down and rise up and take refuge.

Taking Refuge

The world is burning, and if we have any hope of dousing the flames, we need to find ways to resource ourselves and each other.

I have begun to look at the Buddhist teaching of refuge through the lens of the feminine, and the coherence is thrilling me. In Buddhism, taking refuge is a vow, but it's also a treasure, known as the triple gem or the three jewels. We are invited to take refuge in the Buddha, the dharma, and the sangha. Traditionally, to take refuge in the Buddha means to look to the life of the historical Siddhartha Gautama, who became "the Buddha"—the Awakened One—as a role model for living an awakened life. Taking refuge in the dharma implies that it is in the body of teachings the Buddha bequeathed to us that we find the practical tools for living an awakened life. Finally, the sangha is the community of fellow practitioners who accompany you on your journey of awakening.

Let's shift our focus now from a generalized Buddhist perspective to a more universal one and then zero in on an explicitly feminine version of the triple gem. The essential insight at the heart of the concept of taking refuge in the Buddha is that the man known as Siddhartha Gautama showed us what true awakening looks like, right? As it turns out, to awaken mostly means to live with compassion and wisdom, resting in our interconnectedness with all beings, recognizing the truth of suffering, and dedicating ourselves to alleviating it wherever we encounter it. Awakening is our birthright. The Buddha never intended for us to give away our power to him. "Be lamps unto yourselves" were his last words. Yet there are all sorts of role models, lighthouses, campfires available to us, around which we may gather and rest and be fed and wake up.

BUDDHA WOMEN

What would it look like to take refuge in a female version of Ultimate Reality? What if we found our archetypes of awakening among the many women teachers, known and not so well known, across the spiritual traditions and throughout time? While Siddhartha Gautama lived an exemplary life of service, teaching and preaching, a paragon of voluntary simplicity, he was a man, free to do things women cannot. He left his wife and child, for example, to become an ascetic. Jesus too advocated that his followers leave everything and everyone they loved to follow him: "Whoever comes to me and does not hate father and mother, wife and children, brothers and sisters, yes, and even life itself, cannot be my disciple" (Luke 14:26).

Not so simple for a woman (I'm sure it wasn't simple for Siddhartha and Jesus, either, but still). We can certainly choose to leave our kids—and plenty of women have—but we seem to pay a higher price for such a choice than men do. Many of the women mystics we have been exploring here chose to be pilgrims rather than wives, and they had to fight against a prodigious tide in resisting society's expectations and dedicating their lives to prayer. Sometimes their only option for cultivating a spiritual life was to become a nun, even if their inner experience and temperament rendered them unsuited for monasticism. Many, like the bhakti poet Mirabai and the Sufi ecstatic Rabia, embarked on the spiritual quest without either the support or the constraints of the prevailing religious establishment, and they did so at great cost. Independent of any authorities to back them up, they surrendered to a kind of free fall, involving both ecstasy and loneliness.

Let's find the brave women who have walked before us and see how they navigated the journey. Let's investigate female artists, writers, dancers, political leaders, and spiritual teachers who embody qualities we wish to cultivate in ourselves and take refuge in them. Let's lay down our burdens in their metaphysical laps and drink from their ever-flowing breasts.

DHARMA WOMEN

Take refuge in the dharma in the form of teachings by women. Read their love letters to the Holy One. Gaze at their paintings and listen to their musical masterpieces. Study the Christian mystic Catherine of Siena, the Hasidic master Hannah of Ludmir, the heroic Sufi Noor Inayat Khan. Contemplate the Mary Magdalene pieces by the contemporary Irish American poet Marie Howe. Reread the Song of Songs and pay special attention to the Bride. Look at the Hindu classic the Ramayana through the eyes of Sita. Check out powerful voices among young Muslim and indigenous activists like Mona Haydar and Zeina Hashem Beck, Lyla June Johnston and Malala Yousafzai. Engage in Lectio Divina (sacred reading) with their writings. Refill your cup from the wellspring of women's wisdom.

SANGHA WOMEN

Let's take refuge in the companionship of women. When we do not already have a female sangha—a circle that supports one another's awakening whose members happen to be women—we can convene one. We can get together and reflect on the teachings of Julian of Norwich or the Inanna myth. Or meditate in small groups, take silent hikes with women who are willing to join us in quietly communing with Mother Earth. We can draw with pastels, build coiled pots, grind corn and roll tortillas together while listening to the Mexican ballads of Lila Downs or the antiphons of Hildegard of Bingen. We can keep one another accountable to spiritual practice and encourage one another. Let's make ourselves a refuge for one another.

This is the most luminous jewel of all. Sangha. Spiritual companionship. Beloved Vietnamese Zen master Thich Nhat Hanh famously said that the next Buddha (you could substitute Messiah or Christ, Mahdi or White Buffalo Calf Woman) will be the sangha. So have about a million women, only no one was listening. As women, we know this in our brains and in our bellies. We are not waiting for some powerful, supernatural, perfected dude to come along and save us. We look to one another, with all our imperfections and vulnerabilities, our mixed messages and hidden agendas, our startlingly gorgeous and ferociously honest wisdom. Connection *is* liberation. Cultivate it.

deepening

Create an event especially for women on a spiritual path. Maybe it is a silent meditation in solidarity with Syrian refugees or for the restoration of the Amazon rain forest. It could be a writing group using the writing practice methods of Natalie Goldberg (see page 223 for a taste). Perhaps you will be singing sacred chants from one or more spiritual traditions.

Start with a one-time gathering, and if it has legs, run with it and get together on a regular basis. Share leadership. Include food, but only if you can work and eat at the same time; otherwise save the eating for afterward. Blend art and cosmology, political activism and contemplative practice. In other words, let your definition of spiritual community be ample and inclusive. Goddess knows where it will take you.

Love Song to the Great Mother

Beloved One,
Our sister, Mother Earth,
Sacred Woman, Holy Girl,
Crucible of Mercy and Fire of Truth,
Thank you.
We have called and you have come.

You descend on the wings of pain,
The wings of joy,
Bringing solace and vitality.
You rise through the roots of the trees
Spreading shelter, offering refuge.
You enter through the cries of the young
Demanding protection for the vulnerable.

Even as we bow before your beautiful body,
You affirm the beauty of our bodies.
You bless every particle of creation
With your Divine Presence.

We welcome you, who have lived long enough in exile,
To dwell among us again.
We offer ourselves
As your loving stewards,
Your beloved reluctant prophets,
Radiant reflections
Of your own Sacred Self.

Thank you.
Thank you.
And again we give thanks.

Writing Practice Guidelines

Many of the deepening practices I offer in this book are writing exercises. I know of few methods more transformational than writing freely for ten or twenty minutes in response to an evocative prompt.

I encourage you to make a list of your own topics, in addition to the ones I offer in this book, and use them to engage in writing practice sessions on your own or with one or more companions.

Here are some guidelines I adapted from my friend and mentor Natalie Goldberg, best-selling author of *Writing Down the Bones*, *Wild Mind*, and many other books on writing as a spiritual practice.

- Time yourself. Write the topic at the top of the page (or computer screen), and then GO for twenty minutes, without stopping and without censoring yourself.

- Let yourself lose control. Follow your heart and write down whatever arises. Don't worry about being appropriate. Go for authenticity. Let it flow.

- Be specific. It's easy to get lost in philosophical abstractions. Stay grounded. Use embodied language. Not just love, but the smell of your baby's hair. Not only peace, but the rhythm of your own breath as you drop down into the silence.

- Don't ruminate. Take the leash off and let your mind go wherever it's drawn. If the topic is "The Buddha's Tears" and you have a memory of your grandmother's cheese enchiladas, follow that. Your first thoughts will lead you where you need to go.

- Don't worry about punctuation, spelling, or grammar. Experiment with not crossing anything out. Freeing yourself from the rules of conventional language helps liberate you from those limiting inner voices.

- "You are free to write the worst junk in America," says Natalie. Writing practice is not about getting published. It's about gaining access to your own "wild mind."

- "Go for the jugular," Natalie advises. "If something scary comes up, go for it. That's where the energy is." If connecting with this material brings up difficult emotions, gently invite yourself to write through the pain—neither clinging to what arises nor pushing it away, but simply bearing compassionate witness to your own sweet self.

Mystics, Prophets, and Goddesses

Here are some key terms from this book, defined in my own Mirabai language. They may or may not conform to established theology.

- **Mystic**   A person who has a direct experience of the sacred, unmediated by conventional religious rituals or intermediaries, transcending established belief systems, bypassing the intellect, and dissolving identification with the separate (ego) self.

- **Prophet**   A person who answers the call to step up in service to humanity and the earth, even when it is inconvenient and unpopular, and who experiences this calling as sacred.

- **Feminine**   An aggregate of *qualities* such as mercy, loving-kindness, wildness, inclusiveness, radical truth telling and *tendencies* such as nurturing, subversive, relational, community building, heart centered, honoring of embodied experience, comfortable with ambiguity.

- **Feminine mystic**   One whose relationship with the Great Mystery is grounded in the feminine qualities and tendencies listed above. In my experience, "the feminine" is pretty much synonymous with "feminine mystic."

- **Goddess**   An archetypal being who represents certain spiritual attributes to which we may aspire, such as tenderness or ferocity, and also carries a metaphysical energy we can tap into when we need the support of our invisible allies.

- **Divine Masculine**   The sublime aspects of the masculine spiritual paradigm, an inclination toward detachment and transcendence, intellectual clarity and religious rigor, purification and perfection.

- **Patriarchy**   A social or religious system in which men hold the majority of power and women and children are marginalized. These systems are designed, constructed, and operated with men's experience as the default paradigm, while women's experience is not considered or is minimized. Both women and men are harmed by this imbalance.

Acknowledgments

Countless women, from ancient times to the present, have contributed to the flowering of this particular book in this particular moment. As much as I wish I could name each one, it is not possible. And so I offer gratitude for the following, resigned to the fact that I will be leaving out some important friends and teachers.

First, my thanks, as always, to my agent, Sarah Jane Freymann, who is family, really. Sarah Jane, you quietly embody the feminine mystic qualities I am writing about here: loving-kindness balanced by fierce truth telling, generosity of spirit leading to engaged compassion. Thanks to my editor, Joelle Hann, whose attention to detail, coupled with insight grounded in years of her own spiritual practice, surpassed any editorial experience I have ever had. She helped to transfigure this manuscript from a private love poem to the Mother into a universal offering. And to Haven Iverson and Tami Simon, who continue to make a place for me at the Sounds True table: gratitude. You guys are so much more than a publisher; you are my sangha. I was thrilled that Diana Rico, whose own work I have long admired, became my copyeditor. Leslie Brown and Karen Bullock, with her predecessor, Sarah Gorecki, and the entire Sounds True production team ushered this project into the world with care and grace. When Rebecca Mayer stepped in to help secure permissions and prepare endnotes, I thought I had gone to heaven; such professionalism combined with so much love and insight are a rare and precious gift. My assistant, Pouria, is a feminine mystic in the body of a man, who manages many details of my work in the world while ever placing human kindness above business. Thank you, Erin Currier, for your astounding artwork that so masterfully blends spirit and justice, the very essence of what I'm striving for here. I have always wanted a piece of your art, and now it graces my book cover for all time!

Thank you to Stephen Dinan and the incredible team at The Shift network where these teachings have been ripening over the years.

To my daughters, stepdaughters, and grandchildren, thank you for filling my life with delight: Daniela, Kali, Ganga, Yamuna, Jacob, Bree, Niko, Metztli, Sol, Naya, and Aliyah, and the memory of my beloved Jenny. Gratitude to my wise and loving mother, Susanna Starr, and my hilarious and loyal siblings, Amy Starr and Roy Starr, who form the matrix of my life. I cannot imagine myself separate from my belonging to this family. Gratitude to my mother-in-law, Bette Little, who, at nearly one hundred years of age, remains the essence of feisty wisdom and fashion, and to my sisters-in-law, Linda, Marbie, and Lynn, who are steadfast in their commitment to collective healing and awakening.

To my husband, Ganga Das (a.k.a. Jeff), who listened to pretty much every word of this book as it unfolded, keeps the house clean and the food flowing so that I can write my ass off, and makes sure to distract me at the perfect intervals to go have fun. You are the embodiment of the Divine Masculine. I would not have the courage to speak out in this way without the refuge of your embrace.

Deep bow to my lifelong mentors Charlene McDermott, Natalie Goldberg, and Asha Greer. Your wisdom is the well-spring from which these words flow. And to my dharma sisters whose commitment to speaking the authentic voice of the feminine is shifting the paradigm before our eyes: Roshi Joan Halifax, Gangaji, Lama Tsultrim Allione, Caroline Myss, Naomi Shihab Nye, Ann Holmes Redding, Anne Lamott, Dena Merriam, Lama Palden Drolma, Zuleikha, Tamam Kahn, Saraswati Markus, Miranda Macpherson, Beverly Lanzetta, Cynthia Jurs, Camille Helminski, Sera Beak, Cynthia Bourgeault, Devaa Haley Mitchell, Pat McCabe, Dorothy Walters, Rabbi Tirzah Firestone, Eve Ilsen, Laurie Anderson, Sharon Salzberg, Pema Chödrön, Taj Inayat Kahn, Diane Berke, Tessa Bielecki, Rabbi Leah Novick, Sister Greta Ronningen, Yogacharya Ellen Grace

O'Brian, Dr. Clarissa Pinkola Estés, Nina Rao, Ondrea Levine, Mirabai Bush, Dr. Joanne Cacciatore, and so many other women whose wings of wildness and mercy help us all to soar. Thanks to all the people I interviewed, whether or not your words made it to the page, including Lisa "Kishan" Seepaul, Billy Stewart, and Jeannie Zandi.

Boundless gratitude to my lifelong friend and elder guru brother Ram Dass. Your love of the sacred feminine and your intimacy with the world's great wisdom ways have informed all I do and am. Thank you for always checking in to see what I'm writing about, and listening deeply, and affirming my work with the clarity of a sage and the enthusiasm of an uncle!

My friendships with social change agents such as Rev. angel Kyodo Williams, Christena Cleveland, Mona Haydar, and Anita Rodríguez have rocked my world and transfigured it for the better. Even as I was completing this book about the interconnected wisdom of the feminine across the spiritual traditions, my consciousness was undergoing an awakening around white privilege, white spirituality, and questions of unconscious racism, which made me want to recast the whole thing in light of these issues (I didn't). Now that this boat has left the shore, I know I will never be able to return to the land of blissful ignorance of the ways in which the traditions I embrace have been responsible for the suffering of people I love. The adventure continues.

I am grateful to the young women in my life who are stepping up as the brilliant and beautiful prophetic voices we so urgently need and whose work I am honored to support with my love: Mona Haydar, Vera de Chalambert, Lyla June Johnston, Callie Little, Rachel Halder, Ganga Devi Braun, Melanie Moser, Cora Neumann, Jaime Grechika, Phileena Heuertz, Kate Sheehan Roach, Jennifer Alia Wittman, Adriana Rizzolo, LiYana Silver, Ivonne Prieto Rose, and all the women working with such love behind the scenes to share the teachings of Ram Dass and the darshan of Neem Karoli Baba with the world.

My circle of women friends is an unending source of strength, humor, and perspective: Jenny Bird, Tot Tatarsky, Nancy Laupheimer, Tania Casselle, Tara Lupo, Kausalya Karen Pettit, Julie Tato, Brady Hogan, Jean Kenin, Sara Morgan, Susan Berman, Bobbi Shapiro, Kate Rabinowitz, Satrupa Kagel, Toinette Lippe, Kelly Notaras, and many other soul sisters. Each of you contributed to this book in ways you may or may not know about. Your living example of wild mercy enriches my life beyond measure.

And to all the men who have touched my life with your tenderness, your vulnerability, and your willingness to listen deeply and support the feminine, my loving thanks.

Permissions

Thanks for permission to reprint excerpts from the following previously published works:

Excerpts on pages vi and 74 from "Dance, Lalla, with Nothing On," by Lalleshwari, from *Naked Song,* edited by Coleman Barks. Athens, GA: Maypop Books, 1992. Reprinted by permission of Coleman Barks.

Excerpt(s) from *The Interior Castle* by St. Teresa of Ávila, translated by Mirabai Starr, translation copyright © 2003 by Mirabai Starr. Used by permission of Riverhead, an imprint of Penguin Publishing Group, a division of Penguin Random House LLC. All rights reserved. In the UK: From *The Interior Castle* by St. Teresa of Ávila, published by Rider Books. Reproduced by permission of The Random House Group Ltd. © 2003.

Excerpt from *The Sabbath: Its Meaning for Modern Man* by Abraham Joshua Heschel. Copyright © 1951 by Abraham Joshua Heschel, renewed 1979 by Sylvia Heschel. Reprinted by permission of Farrar, Straus and Giroux.

Rumi, "The Song of the Reed," translated by Kabir Helminski and Camille Helminski, from *The Rumi Collection*, edited by Kabir Helminski. Copyright © 1998 by Kabir Helminski. Reprinted by arrangement with The Permissions Company, Inc., on behalf of Shambhala Publications, Inc., Boulder Colorado, shambhala.com.

Excerpt from *Teresa of Ávila: The Book of My Life*, translated by Mirabai Starr, © 2007 by Mirabai Starr. Reprinted by arrangement with The Permissions Company, Inc., on behalf of New Seeds Books, an imprint of Shambhala Publications, Inc., Boulder, Colorado, shambhala.com.

About the Author

Mirabai Starr writes creative nonfiction and contemporary translations of sacred literature. She taught Philosophy and World Religions at the University of New Mexico-Taos for twenty years and now teaches and speaks internationally on contemplative practice, compassionate action, and the teachings of the mystics across the spiritual traditions. Mirabai has received critical acclaim for her revolutionary new translations of John of the Cross, Teresa of Ávila, and Julian of Norwich. She is the award-winning author of *God of Love: A Guide to the Heart of Judaism, Christianity, and Islam*, which positions her at the forefront of the emerging interspiritual movement, and *Caravan of No Despair: A Memoir of Loss and Transformation*, a book about the extraordinary coinciding of the publication of her first book, *Dark Night of the Soul*, with the sudden death of her beloved daughter Jenny. Mirabai has been teaching online courses about women mystics and goddesses with The Shift Network since 2013. With *Wild Mercy*, Mirabai offers the fruit of decades of study, teaching, and contemplative practice in a fresh, slightly subversive, lyrical voice to a growing circle of women and men thirsty for the life-giving essence of feminine wisdom. She lives with her extended family in the mountains of northern New Mexico.

About Sounds True

Sounds True is a multimedia publisher whose mission is to inspire and support personal transformation and spiritual awakening. Founded in 1985 and located in Boulder, Colorado, we work with many of the leading spiritual teachers, thinkers, healers, and visionary artists of our time. We strive with every title to preserve the essential "living wisdom" of the author or artist. It is our goal to create products that not only provide information to a reader or listener, but that also embody the quality of a wisdom transmission.

For those seeking genuine transformation, Sounds True is your trusted partner. At SoundsTrue.com you will find a wealth of free resources to support your journey, including exclusive weekly audio interviews, free downloads, interactive learning tools, and other special savings on all our titles.

To learn more, please visit SoundsTrue.com/freegifts or call us toll-free at 800.333.9185.